# HEART
# TALK

# HEART
# TALK

POETIC WISDOM FOR <sup>A BETTER</sup> LIFE

# CLEO
# WADE

37INK

—

**ATRIA**

New York ♥ London ♥ Toronto ♥ Sydney ♥ New Delhi

## 37INK

ATRIA

An Imprint of Simon & Schuster, Inc.

1230 Avenue of the Americas

New York, NY 10020

First 37INK/Atria Books hardcover edition March 2018

37INK / **ATRIA** BOOKS and colophon are trademarks of Simon & Schuster, Inc.

For information about special discounts for bulk purchases, please contact Simon & Schuster Special Sales at 1-866-506-1949 or business@simonandschuster.com.

The Simon & Schuster Speakers Bureau can bring authors to your live event. For more information or to book an event, contact the Simon & Schuster Speakers Bureau at 1-866-248-3049 or visit our website at www.simonspeakers.com.

Interior design by Laura Palese

Manufactured in the United States of America

10 9 8 7 6

Library of Congress Cataloging-in-Publication Data

Names: Wade, Cleo, author.

Title: Heart talk : poetic wisdom for a better life / Cleo Wade.

Description: New York, NY : Atria / 37 INK, 2018. |

Identifiers: LCCN 2017057816 (print) | LCCN 2017061566 (ebook) | ISBN 9781501177354 | ISBN 9781501177347 (paperback) | ISBN 9781501191138

Subjects: LCSH: Self-realization. | Self-realization—Poetry. | Conduct of life. | Conduct of life—Poetry. | BISAC: POETRY / Inspirational & Religious. | SELF-HELP / Personal Growth / General. | BODY, MIND & SPIRIT / Inspiration & Personal Growth.

Classification: LCC BJ1470 (ebook) | LCC BJ1470 .W33 2018 (print) | DDC 158.1—dc23

LC record available at https://lccn.loc.gov/2017057816

ISBN 978-1-5011-9113-8

ISBN 978-1-5011-7735-4 (ebook)

This is dedicated
to every human being
who looks different, feels different,
and thinks differently.
I see you. I feel you. I am you.
Stay different. Our world needs
the difference we will make.

Dearest You,

I have experienced just about every type of heartbreak that exists. The kind that happens with a romantic partner, with someone I wished were a romantic partner, with a family member, a friend, even a stranger. I've known the heartbreak associated with professional situations and things I aspire to: a dream that never came true, or a dream that did come true, but when it did, it wasn't meant to be. I have even broken my own heart a few times (more than a few, actually).

What I have learned from having my heart in pieces is that our stories are important. They help us take our pieces and build something new. And if we build with love they can help us build something even better than we had before.

When we get real and honest and raw about what we go through, we have the power to turn our words into medicine and our experiences into wisdom.

This book is a compilation of notes I have written in my apartment in New York City. It also consists of poems about loving, being, and healing that have been my life rafts when I did not know how to swim in the waters of the world. You will also find the type of good ol'-fashioned heartfelt advice I would share with you if we were sitting in my home at my kitchen table (by the way, thanks, Mom, for showing me the healing power of kitchen-table conversation).

I hope that in reading this book you will be reminded of your strength, reintroduced to your resilience, and reconnected with your personal power and love of self.

And if you would like to treat this book less like a book and more like a friend or a companion, I would like that very much.

Also, you should know that I love you. I don't need to know you to love you. If this pile of papers found its way into your life, it is because we are meant to be. You are my tribe, and I am yours.

If you have any questions, complaints, new ideas, love notes, or invitations for tea, I am here for you, talk to me: HeartTalk@cleowade.com.

Love,
Cleo

PS: Along the way, you will find that I have written some notes in the margins throughout this book. I did this in hopes that you'll feel welcomed to not treat this book too preciously. Write in it, rip out a page and pin it on the fridge, read it front to back, or pick a page to read at random when you need a moment to yourself to recharge. Let these words show up for you however you'd like. No rules.

# HEART
## TALK

GET HONEST WITH YOURSELF.
BE THE PERSON YOU
ARE THE CLEAREST WITH.

BE THE PERSON YOU ARE
THE MOST FEARLESS WITH.

THESE ARE THE SEEDS
THAT TURN YOUR LIFE
INTO A GARDEN OF
AUTHENTICITY.

# FIRST THINGS FIRST:

## SELF - CARE.

Self-care is how we fuel our self-love so that we are able to share our love with everyone around us. Our hearts are warm when we are able to show up with generosity, patience, and compassion for the ones we love, but we must remember that it is impossible to truly be there for others without taking care of ourselves first. We take care of ourselves by asking what our needs are. We take care of ourselves by making healthy choices when it comes to our physical and emotional bodies. We take care of ourselves by lightening up and not being so damn hard on ourselves. At times, life seems to be one never-ending to-do list, but we must learn to disrupt the flood of life's demands in order to replenish our energy so that we can fully show up for all of our passions and responsibilities. It does not benefit anyone when we live our lives running on fumes. Love is an action, a thing in motion. There-fore, it requires fuel. ᴡ

ONLY A FULL TANK CAN GO THE DISTANCE.

# hiding and seeking

when I let go
of who
I thought I had to be
I could
finally
and powerfully
become who
I really am
oh,
to find out
I had been hiding
and did not know that
(self-)love
had been looking
for me
all along

YOU WANT TO
FIND LOVE?
    LOSE YOUR FEAR.


YOU WANT TO
STAY IN LOVE?
    LOSE YOUR EGO.

How many times have we let our fear of getting hurt or disappointed keep us from love? Love requires us to unpack our fear and pain so those feelings do not interfere with our ability to thrive in connection with others. This process requires a level of bravery, vulnerability, and intimacy that can be scary and deeply uncomfortable, but real love only exists outside of our comfort zone. We can only step into love when we leave our fear behind. To be fearless is to be afraid of something but to do it anyway. Be fearless. Take the first step. Once we choose love, the work to maintain our love begins. The first step in this is conquering our ego. A loving relationship is built on compromise and working with our partner to continuously evolve into our best selves. This is not possible without hard truths, tough conversations, personal growth, and behavioral shifts. The ego does not like any of this. The ego wants us to believe that we are always right and that our way of doing things is always the best way. Our spirit, on the other hand, knows that the people we love are in our life to challenge us to rise to new levels of consideration and care in all that we do. We cannot truly choose to invest in love while our ego is present, for real love runs on *selflessness*, and the ego runs on *selfishness*. ⚘

AND THE BEST NEWS
OF ALL IS THAT IT IS
NEVER TOO LATE TO
BECOME THE PERSON
YOU'VE ALWAYS
WANTED TO BE.

Take a deep breath and go for it. Don't allow the energy of procrastination to create a staleness surrounding your dreams. Breath is a sign of the body living. When you inhale deeply, you are reminded that you are alive and that every moment represents a new possibility for you to step into your destiny. 〜

DON'T BE THE ONE YOU ARE WAITING ON.

## it's only natural

of course
I've changed,
darling . . .
I've grown.

Change is necessary. It is important. And it is also what makes life exciting. When we fear change, it keeps us in an energy of feeling stuck, powerless, and resentful, but when we embrace change, we open ourselves to the understanding that anything is possible. Life is not supposed to stay the same. We are not supposed to stay the same. Our life, our communities, and our world are always in bloom. When we understand this, we see that change is growth, and growth is essential for each of us to reach our individual and collective potential. ⋎

## all of it

which parts of yourself won't you let yourself
love yet?

befriend your ingredients

the spicy, the sweet, the pain, the heartache, the gifts, the shame,
and the shine

fall
in love
with
*all*
of you

savor
yourself

cleo wade

FOUR STEPS FOR OPENING YOURSELF
UP TO A MORE RADICAL LIFE:

1. LOVE YOURSELF ENOUGH TO GET
   TO KNOW YOURSELF.

2. ACHIEVE STEP ONE BY HAVING
   THE COURAGE TO ASK YOURSELF
   THE HARD QUESTIONS.

3. HONOR STEP TWO BY HAVING
   THE COURAGE TO ANSWER THE
   HARD QUESTIONS.

4. REPEAT STEPS 1-3 YOUR
   WHOLE LIFE.

## KNOWING YOUR NEEDS IS A SUPERPOWER.

Our world often tells us that there is something wrong with needing something or someone, or that expressing our needs is somehow a sign of weakness. This is completely untrue. Knowing our needs is a limitless superpower, one that can help us make all the big decisions in life. When we know what we need from a partner, we spend much less time dating the wrong people. When we know what we need to feel challenged and motivated by our work, we are much more tuned in to what we want our career path to look like. And when we know what we need in order to be our best selves, we are much better at showing up as that person in our relationships with our friends and family. Be unapologetic when it comes to your needs. They are, at the very least, deserving of being seen and heard. What are your needs? Create a list of your needs and make space for them in your life. Respecting and expressing your needs can super-power your life. Start by recognizing them. ❧

WE MAY NOT ALWAYS HAVE THE
POWER TO CONTROL WHAT SHOWS
UP AT OUR DOOR, BUT WE
ALWAYS, ALWAYS, ALWAYS HAVE THE
POWER TO DECIDE WHAT STAYS
AND WHAT GOES.

No matter how much work we do on ourselves,
stress and anxiety will still show up. Our work is not
to avoid them; it isn't to wrestle with them or "cope"
with them. Stress and anxiety are unavoidable

visitors. Let us accept this. When they come, acknowledge their arrival, evaluate what invited them in, and recognize that they are guests, not permanent fixtures. They will leave, especially if we don't entertain them or pick a fight with them. No matter how overwhelming the feelings that come with stress and anxiety are, we must always remember that we are human, and though we may not be able to control their arrival, we always have the power to release them. Pause. Breathe slowly and deliberately. Think positively. Remember your strength. These feelings will eventually leave, because ultimately they know they have no home within your sacred self. ❧

# YES? YES. YES!

We spend so much of our lives hearing others tell us to go after what we want, but few speak to the anxiety that often comes once we actually get what we want. We cannot have our dreams if we do not learn to say yes to them. Achieving our goals and desires is only as powerful as our ability to receive them. We are all familiar with the act of standing in our own way. Sometimes it is because we are scared: You are in the final interview of your dream job and all of a sudden you start thinking, "Can I really do this?" Or you finally meet the romantic partner that you know you deserve and then ask yourself, "Am I worthy?" Yes. You can do it. Yes. You are worthy. Move out of your own way and say yes to yourself and yes to the world. Say yes. In fact, don't just say yes . . . celebrate your yes. It is a victory. ❦

## it was time

so I said yes
I said yes to living
I said yes to loving
I said yes to being
my . . .
self
illuminated
and unafraid

LET GO OF SHAME.

IT WILL NOT ADD

A SINGLE SMILE,

DOLLAR, OR MINUTE

TO YOUR LIFE.

## love never lies

shame never tells
the truth
it tells you
you are not
good enough
the truth is
you are
it tells you
you have to be perfect
the truth is
you don't
it tells you
your mistakes
are fatal wounds
the truth is
you heal
it tells you
everything has fallen apart
the truth is
you will rebuild
it tells you
that you will stay sunken in despair
the truth is
you will rise

it tells you
you failed
you lost
& you got hurt
the truth is
you learned (what to do next time)
you gained (knowledge from your
knockdown)
& you found out (just how strong you
are)
it says
you will never make it
the truth is
keep going
for
shame said
you would never
survive
and the truth is
you
are
still
here

# NOT EVERY GROUND IS A BATTLE-GROUND▶

Wise soldiers know that not every ground is a battleground. Their scars do not let them forget that they have had to be a fighter, but their scars also do not let them forget that the human body cannot live every day in the trenches. To exist in a state that requires you to constantly be prepared to go to war is exhausting. No human body or soul can sustain that type of energy as a lifestyle. Let yourself relax. The ground is not only the place where we march toward what we must fight for; it is also a place where we are being <u>divinely</u> held up by the earth. ⚘

GRATITUDE IS A SPIRITUAL

AND ECONOMICAL

FORM OF STRESS RELIEF.

cleo wade

Learning the power of gratitude is not only wise, it is practical. When we understand how to feel grateful for what we have, we are free from the uneasy state of constantly wanting. A never-ending hunt for more puts the mind in a continual state of anxiety. But when we are thankful for what we have and understand the difference between what we want and what we need, we are able to relax the mind and put less pressure on ourselves to obsessively upgrade the things in our life. Release the energy of more, more, more and replace it with the energy of thank you, thank you, thank you. 🌱

IF YOU AREN'T STAYING IN THE MOMENT, YOU ARE LEAVING IT.

My brother once said to me, "If you are not staying present in the moment, you are leaving it." Those words really struck me. They made me realize that if I did not develop a practice of staying present, I would spend my entire life leaving wherever I was. The only way we can make the most of our lives is to make the most of our moments. Today, wherever you are, decide to stay. We can know the gifts that lie in the present only if we stay in it long enough to receive them. ▾

SOMETIMES THE
BEST PRESENT
IS BEING
PRESENT.

IF YOU WANT TO FEEL EMPOWERED
BY ALL OF YOUR DECISIONS, YOU
CAN'T JUST CALCULATE YOUR RISKS.
YOU HAVE TO FULLY AND TOTALLY
ACCEPT YOUR RISKS AS WELL.

cleo wade

When we apply the energy of acceptance to risk-taking, we are able to take risks with much more confidence and steadiness. Acceptance is when we bring trust to a situation. We all take risks, but if we want to master risk-taking, we must learn to do so without attaching anxious energy to our decisions. Anxiety disconnects us from our power. Acceptance allows us to relax into our power and move through any circumstance with clarity and confidence. ❦

TAKE RISKS WITH FAITH, NOT FEAR.

MAY ALL OF
YOUR VIBES SAY:

I GOT THIS.

Confidence is not something we have, it is something we practice so that it lives in flow with all that we do. Confidence is not something we have by saying "Okay, I need to be confident right now." True confidence comes from affirming ourselves regularly and treating ourselves kindly. When our mental chatter props us up and reminds us that we are capable of whatever we wish to accomplish, half of the battle of achieving any goal is already won. Don't approach your life from a space of defeat. Approach your life with the vibrancy of "I got this," because at the end of the day . . . who is to say you don't? ❦

When we live with honesty, positive intentions, fairness, love, integrity, and transparency, we do not need to spend our time explaining ourselves to others. Explanations are necessary only when our actions require justifications, and justifications are necessary only when our intentions are murky. Live your life with clear and good intentions and you will never have to spend your time explaining what you do or who you are. ⚘

# I choose to shine

what is within us
appears before us
when I
think like
a cactus too long
I am all of a sudden
a cactus
I am in the desert
I am without water
and not even
the one I love
can
touch me
so I think
like the sun instead
and
nourish
the growth of
all
with my
light
and my
warmth

CLEAN OUT YOUR THOUGHTS —

THEY HAVE THE POWER TO COVER

YOUR ENTIRE LIFE IN DIRT.

Healthy thinking is when we choose to guide our thoughts in a way that benefits our best self. Every thought, especially our repetitive thoughts, manifests itself in our lives. For example, if we are stuck in a thought cycle of "I am not good enough," we will start to see the outside world affirm that thought. We may also find our behavior begin to affirm that thought when we isolate ourselves from the people in our lives who love us and know that we are good enough. Since our thoughts are what frame our lives, the first step to constructing a healthy life is to construct healthy thoughts. Healthy thinking does not mean you never have dark thoughts; it just means that you don't stay in unhelpful thoughts long enough for them to influence your reality. We become the stories we tell ourselves, so it is crucial that we, as narrators, frame our experiences with thoughts that heal, nurture, and motivate us. We are more in charge of our thoughts than we think. Keep your inner world loving and hopeful, and your outside world will begin to reflect exactly that. ❦

LOVE YOUR-SELF ENOUGH

Love yourself enough to walk into only the rooms and situations that show care and love for you. Love yourself enough to walk out of the rooms that harm you in any way. Love yourself enough to hold the people who harm you accountable for their words and actions. Love yourself enough to express your wants, your needs, and your desires. Love yourself enough to tell the truth. Love yourself enough to keep yourself safe. Love yourself enough to say enough is enough when enough has become enough. ༷

A LOVE LIKE THIS MOVES MOUNTAINS.

## be heard

sing your song

if that is what
is inside of you
sing
your
damn
song

do
your soul
that
favor

You are the only person who truly decides who you are. If you want to be a singer . . . think like a singer, say you are a singer, and of course sing your song. We spend so much of our lives waiting for others to qualify us. Authorize *yourself.* Step into your power right now; give yourself your own credentials, and *you* be the one who qualifies who you are. Why not? Nobody knows you better than you do. 🌱

BE KIND.
IT SHAKES THE WORLD.

cleo wade

There is no way to give kindness to another without knowing it in ourselves first. We must continually ask ourselves (especially on our tough days when we are feeling the most hurt or irritated): Is this the kindest thought I could have? Is this the kindest thing I could say? Is this the kindest action I could take in this situation? To achieve a kinder world, we must approach kindness with ambition and dedication. We must practice it in every moment of our lives. Kindness is that important. ☜

JUST A FRIENDLY REMINDER:
NOTHING ABOUT YOU IS A MISTAKE.
YOU ARE A GIFT AND YOU ARE HERE
FOR A REASON. YOU DESERVE
TO TAKE UP SPACE IN THE
WORLD, AND WE NEED YOU HERE.

cleo wade

## stand tall

the tree never
feels less like a tree
because it is different
from the others
in the forest

so why would *we* ever think we are meant to all be the same?

to be unique is to be a living thing

KNOW THE VALUE OF
KNOWING YOUR VALUE.

Some of the best advice I ever received was when my first mentor at my first real job in New York City told me, "Don't wait on anyone to tell you what you are worth. You have to be the first person who knows what you are worth and can say what you are worth." I have always kept that advice close to me when navigating the waters of not only my work but also my personal relationships. In the world of work, you have to be the first one who knows the value of your talents and also the first one who can express what you are worth to your boss, client, or collaborator. Similarly, in the world of dating and relationships, you have to be the first one to tell another person how your time and energy deserve to be treated. When we know our value and can express our value, we are able to teach others how to honor what we bring to the table. ✱

WHAT WE DO AND HOW WE SPEAK
IS EITHER CONSTRUCTIVE OR
DESTRUCTIVE. CHOOSE TO BE
CONSTRUCTIVE. DON'T BE A
BULLDOZER WHERE LIFE CALLS
ON YOU TO BE A BUILDER.

Very few decisions in life leave us in a neutral space. Most of the decisions we make when it comes to work, family, and relationships are either constructive or destructive. Ask yourself: Which are you choosing? Is the way you treat your loved one building your bond or breaking it apart? Does your behavior toward them chip away at your trust or solidify it? How are you treating yourself? The body, mind, and spirit require constructive thoughts and actions in order to build your best possible life. Don't tear yourself down when you have the power to build yourself up. ☙

# I did not lose the lesson

I did a lot of things
not in the right way
some may even call them
mistakes

I just call them
the scars
that keep me
from touching the oven
too long
when it is hot

cleo wade

Life does not always hand us the easy road. Life does not always allow for us to be in the right frame of mind to always do the right thing at the right time. To know this is to remember that you are human. We are not born knowing the best way to navigate the worst circumstances. We are all more than our mistakes. Our mistakes do not make us bad people. Our mistakes, when met with awareness and personal responsibility, are actually what introduce us to our best selves. You are beautiful because of all of your experiences—the good, the bad, and the imperfect. 🌱

## how to keep going

pause
breathe
repair your universe
proceed

WE ALL REQUIRE HEALING AT
ONE POINT OR ANOTHER. TAKE
TIME TO HEAL YOUR WOUNDS.
TAKE TIME TO HEAL YOUR
HEART. IT DOES NO GOOD
TO THINK ABOUT RUNNING
THE MARATHON WHEN YOU
STILL HAVE A BROKEN FOOT.

MAYBE DON'T DO THINGS

THE WAY YOU HAVE

ALWAYS DONE THEM

SIMPLY BECAUSE THAT

IS THE WAY YOU HAVE

ALWAYS DONE THEM.

cleo wade

There can be no flow without the spirit of flexibility. Allow yourself to be flexible. When we walk into situations feeling so sure of who we are and what we know, we are unable to create space for others or for our own personal growth. When we are flexible, we open ourselves to mountains of possibilities, new ideas, and revelations. To be in flow means to be able to move through the world with the ability to roll with whatever comes up. There is no way to do this if the energy you embody is rigid and stubborn. Loosen up. ❦

## a release

I am holding on
but
my hands are tired
and
turning red
this had me thinking
maybe to love
I had to
let go
instead

Is what you are holding on to taking all of your energy? Are your hands clenched, your body tight, and your soul strained? Whether it is in the realm of your job, your family dynamic, or your romantic relationship, know that just because something is important to us, does not mean we have to control it by attaching stress, worry, and anxiety to it. Let go. Let what is meant to be . . . be. What is meant for us flows freely in harmony with us, not against us. ⋎

REMEMBER NOT TO

CARE ABOUT THE THINGS

YOU DON'T EVEN

CARE ABOUT.

cleo wade

Sometimes our habitual thinking takes over and we end up complaining or being upset about things that don't actually matter to us. Break the habit. Before you get worked up about something, ask yourself, *Do I really value this enough to exhaust myself emotionally over it?* Ask yourself if it is worth it to have it play on a mental loop in your head. Ask yourself if it is worth your energy or worth your words. You are in charge of how much space a thought takes up in your life. Take the time to carefully consider what you let be a part of your being and your spirit. ⚘

## a message from today

maybe
don't
tomorrow
your
life
away

THE BEST THING ABOUT YOUR
LIFE IS THAT IT IS CONSTANTLY
IN A STATE OF DESIGN.
THIS MEANS YOU HAVE,
AT ALL TIMES, THE POWER TO
REDESIGN IT. MAKE MOVES,
ALLOW SHIFTS, SMILE MORE,
DO MORE, DO LESS, SAY NO,
SAY YES — JUST REMEMBER,
WHEN IT COMES TO YOUR LIFE,
YOU ARE NOT ONLY THE ARTIST
BUT THE MASTERPIECE AS WELL.

IF YOU ARE GRATEFUL FOR WHERE

YOU ARE, YOU HAVE TO RESPECT

THE ROAD THAT GOT YOU THERE.

We must appreciate all that we survive: the small, the medium, and the monumental. Find gratitude in your life story. Wake up every morning and say to yourself, "I made it here from where I started, and I am so proud of that." When we do this, we bless ourselves and feed ourselves with the love required for us to flourish and keep going no matter where we come from or what we have been through. ❦

GENEROSITY NEVER THINKS
PAST THE PRESENT MOMENT.
GENEROSITY IS WHEN
YOU GIVE WHAT YOU CAN GIVE
AND DO WHAT YOU CAN DO
LIKE THERE IS NO TOMORROW.

## doing what you can with what you've got

and even when
I had not a
penny in my pocket
I still knew the joy of giving

I gave my time
I gave my spirit
I gave my heart

I gave myself fully to the moment
and
even through my tears
I gave my smile to the world
(it needed it more than I could have ever imagined)

WHEN WE OVERCOME OUR FEAR OF
FAILING, WE HAVE THE POWER TO
STEP INTO THE MAGNIFICENCE
OF OUR RESILIENCE. DO THE THINGS
YOU ARE AFRAID TO DO.
DO THE THINGS THAT FEEL BIG.
DO THE THINGS THAT SHOW YOU
WHAT YOU ARE MADE OF.

cleo wade

The people we admire for exhibiting excellence are not the people who are perfect or the people who succeed every time. They are the people who recognize that the road to achieving every goal is paved with victory *and* defeat. The triumphant are celebrated not because they win every time but because they never quit when they lose. We are more resilient than we could ever imagine. Keep going. ❦

YOU WANT LOVE?
BE LOVE.

YOU WANT LIGHT?
BE LIGHT.

When you throw a lit match into a fire, the two separate lights never fail to find each other and join as one. This is the same with the energy of love. Love always detects the energy of love, and light never fails to join forces with more light. When we are in a state of positive and loving energy, the whole room feels it; maybe even the whole world feels it. Embody love and light with actions and thoughts that are positive, uplifting, caring, and considerate, and you will find that you attract others who do the same. ⚘

YOUR LIFE EXPERIENCES
ARE ONLY AS VALUABLE
AS YOUR ABILITY TO
TURN THEM INTO
LIFE LESSONS.

cleo wade

We cannot always control what happens to us, but we always have the power to leave any situation feeling stronger and wiser than we were before. There is an education waiting for us within all of our experiences, we just have to decide what we do with it. Choose to allow what you go through to fuel your growth rather than stunt it. ♥

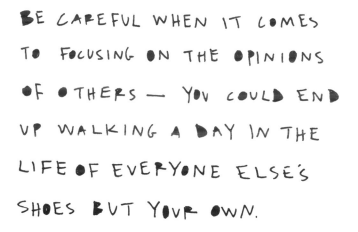

BE CAREFUL WHEN IT COMES
TO FOCUSING ON THE OPINIONS
OF OTHERS — YOU COULD END
UP WALKING A DAY IN THE
LIFE OF EVERYONE ELSE'S
SHOES BUT YOUR OWN.

It is a gift in life to have loving friends, family, and

other types of support as sounding boards when

you are in crisis or in need of help or advice, but

remember to balance the opinions of others with your own inner wisdom. No one knows your life the way you do, so while we must always ask for help when we need it and show gratitude for advice from others, we must also know the difference between respectfully considering someone's opinion and giving it the power to dictate our lives. We are here to do things in our own style, make our own mistakes, and learn our own lessons in our own unique way. Do not ignore your intuition. There is an infinite intelligence within you; let it be your guiding light. ✌

CREATE YOUR OWN
FINISH LINES. LET
THERE BE AS MANY
AS YOU WANT, AND
LET THERE BE MANY.

To know that you are a work in progress means to recognize that your goals are also works in progress. A friend of mine once said to me that there is no . . . "there." It reminded me that every single day we are growing into who we will be tomorrow. Because we go through so many stages and phases, it is important to consistently reset our goals so that they can grow with us. When we reset our goals, we allow for each one to flow into the next and connect with all phases of our life. Refresh your goals regularly and with intention. It will help you stay continuously motivated and inspired. ❦

THERE IS
NO . . .
"THERE."

## what I lost and what I gained

and then I realized
that to be
more alive
I had to
be
less afraid
so
I did it
I lost my
fear
and gained
my
whole life

ALLOW TODAY TO BE FEARLESS.
WHAT DOES YOUR DAY LOOK LIKE
WITHOUT FEAR? WHAT ARE
THE WORDS YOU ARE HOLDING
BACK BECAUSE OF FEAR?
WHAT ARE THE DREAMS YOU
ARE NOT MAKING INTO
REALITY BECAUSE OF FEAR?
FREE YOURSELF OF THOSE
FEARS. GIVE YOURSELF A
CHANCE TO SEE WHAT YOU
CAN REALLY DO.

AND BE SURE TO KEEP YOUR LIGHT
BRIGHT AND SHINING — YOU NEVER
KNOW JUST HOW MANY PEOPLE
YOU MAY BE A LIGHTHOUSE FOR.
YOU NEVER KNOW HOW MANY
PEOPLE FIND THEIR WAY HOME,
IN EVEN THE WILDEST STORMS,
BECAUSE YOU ARE THERE.

Light is always light no matter the vessel. Do not put pressure on yourself to shine in a specific form. Light can be big, small, loud, or a whisper, but it is always light. Allow your light to take its own shape and shine in its own way. When we embody our own unique light, we have the power to bring healing energy and clarity to any situation. Light allows us to see things for what they are so that we may proceed with understanding, compassion, and grace. We can navigate our journey with much more confidence when we see the world through the light we shine on it. ❦

## what truth will do

and
are we so
scared
that the truth
will hurt us
that we
are willing to
never give it
the opportunity
to
let it
teach us
motivate us
inspire us
heal us
&
maybe
just maybe
free us
too

The best and the worst thing about the truth is that it gets instant results. Do not let fear of what it will reveal keep you from it. Go after it. Let it liberate you. Allow it to give you the gift of clarity so you may move through your life on a more focused and deliberate path. ❦

SOMETIMES THE ONLY THING
ANOTHER PERSON NEEDS IS
FOR US TO BELIEVE IN THEM.

cleo wade

Letting someone know that you believe in them is one of the most fundamental acts of kindness. Be that person for someone. Each person's life is so much more difficult than we could ever imagine. You never know if your words of support could be the sign someone is looking for to feel capable enough to commit to their own greatness. 🌱

FIND SOMEONE

BE THEIR ROCK

(KEEP THEM GROUNDED)

BE THEIR NORTH STAR

(HELP THEM FIND THEIR WAY)

LET

THEM

BE THIS

TO YOU

TOO

Create a sacred space for your relationships by attending to them with trust, love, care, kindness, and support. When we set an intention that the energy between ourselves and someone else is a compassionate, judgment-free zone, we make it possible to be loving shelters for one another. Most people in life are just looking for a safe place to be themselves. When we give that to another person and allow them to give that to us as well, it is a way of keeping each other warm even on life's coldest days. ❦

Best friends give loving and sound advice. Best friends cheer for you. Best friends support you as you grow and evolve. Best friends don't let you beat up on yourself. Best friends show you care and compassion. Best friends show up for you not just when you need it most but also in small, thoughtful, day-to-day ways. Most of us are very good at being a best friend to someone else, but what about being one to ourselves? Are we able to reflect inward and give ourselves advice on a troubling situation? Are we able to cheer for ourselves when we take a risk? Are we able to tell ourselves that it is okay when we feel vulnerable as we grow and evolve out of our comfort zones? Are we able to take care of ourselves when stress is ailing our bodies and spirits? Are we able to do the small things that uplift our mood as we go through the day? Learn to become your own best friend. Share yourself with others, but don't forget to give the best of who you are to yourself as well. You are with yourself for as long as you live . . . so it is probably wise to get good at being a best friend to yourself. ⋎

## owned by you alone

your peace
belongs to you alone
only you
can give it
to yourself
and only you
can take it away

# where to find it

kept looking for goodness
kept asking everyone
where I could find the
good in the world
it was not
until I
looked within
and
grew
my own
goodness
that I
began
to see it
everywhere.

PART OF BEING
UNDERSTOOD IS
MAKING YOURSELF
UNDERSTOOD.

Live with intention. Before you do something, ask yourself why. Ask yourself what you want. Ask yourself why you want it. Ask yourself how you want to feel and how you want to live. Investigate. The clarity of knowing what you care about and what motivates you helps you to be better at allowing those things to guide your decision-making. We can often find ourselves where we don't want to be because our goals or sense of self have gotten hijacked by fear-based opportunity-seeking, pressure from others, or our own insecurities. Gift yourself the confidence to be clear about what you want, to be tapped into your driving purpose, and to know the source of your ambitions. Connect to your internal compass; let the integrity of your core values lead you onward and upward. ⚹

*NO ONE WILL EVER BE BETTER AT COMMUNICATING ON YOUR BEHALF THAN YOU. BE HONEST. BE BRAVE. BE CLEAR. BE DIRECT.

YOU DESERVE YOUR DREAMS —

WHO ELSE COULD THEY POSSIBLY

BELONG TO MORE THAN YOU?

Knowing what we deserve gets us one step closer to having it. Every thought, vision, and idea that frequently occurs in our psyche happens for a reason. Our dreams are our destiny's way of communicating with us. We spend far too much of our time looking at our dreams through the veils of the challenges that live between us and our desires. When we approach our dreams with the energy that says "I can, I will, and I am deserving," we are not only much more likely to attain them, we are also able to better enjoy the road that leads us to them. ❧

When we lead with love, we give strength and care to ourselves and others in a way that can transform any situation. It is only the walls of fear, pain, and insecurity that trap us into believing love cannot conquer all. When we work to let down those walls and connect to the DNA of our basic goodness, we are free to lead with love. Those who lead with love live with fairness, empathy, and patience, doing so without conditions, judgment, or discrimination. When we employ those qualities, we are able to navigate even life's most difficult challenges. Lead with love, you will never regret it. ❦

OUR WORK ETHIC

DOES NOT JUST BELONG

AT WORK.

Our work ethic is something that must be applied to our home, our family, our community, and our world. Don't allow for your goals to exist only in the workplace or where they can be financially rewarded. Live with ambition for your entire existence. Every aspect of your life can be made better with your hard work, love, and devotion. ❧

## turn the lock

the past
cannot stay
the past
if
it is always
on your
mind
there is
only one
person
holding the
key
that frees you
from the shackles
of
days gone by

*you.*

# the way out and the way forward

I loved myself
through what I had
been through

this is how

I stayed afloat
even when
life's waters
raised above my head

and when I needed
someone to trust

this is how I knew
which hands
were helping hands
and which

were hurting hands

## the only battle

I had been
so focused
on winning
and losing
I did not realize
the only battle
was the one
between me and
myself
*for*
myself

When we allow for our wins in life to let us feel like we are on top of the world, we give equal power to allowing our losses to make us feel like the weight of the world is on our shoulders. We can enjoy our successes with less ego and more generosity by remembering that our purpose lies in what we bring to the world, not from the accolades the world brings to us. When we focus solely on validations from the outside world, we end up being very easily controlled by circumstance, but when we remain humble and firmly rooted in our ever-present goodness, we can celebrate our accomplishments and learn from our disappointments without letting them be the things that define us. ⚘

## these things take time

I am
the caterpillar right now
I may not be flying high
like a butterfly
but
I am
sure as hell

grounded

cleo wade

Divine timing is real. The caterpillar enjoys the energy of being grounded as much as it will enjoy the energy of being a butterfly in the sky. This is because one cannot exist without the other, and every phase of the cycle is equally as necessary as the next. You will have less worry in your life when you can appreciate all of the moments of becoming who you are.

DON'T JUST APPRECIATE IT — ENJOY IT.

Complaining is something that seems to come so easy and so naturally to us, but the problem is: complaints have no magic. They don't make anyone's day better, and they don't help any situation. Try going on a complaint cleanse. Monitor when complaints pop into your mind, and instead of saying them out loud, let them go. When we do this, we allow for our language to be part of how we make the world more magical and more peaceful. ⋎

# YOU ARE MORE OKAY THAN YOU THINK.

## as I go forward

I may stumble
but
I stand up
more
than I fall
down

We spend so much of our time focusing on our missteps. When we trip and fall, we seem to only obsess over the ten seconds we were on the ground rather than the rest of our day spent walking perfectly fine. Similarly, in life, we let one heavy moment, month, or year get in the way of our ability to see that we are okay so much more than we are not okay. Falling down does not make us who we are. Standing up does. Rising and continuing to move forward does. ☙

NO ONE'S DAY IS WHAT
YOU THINK IT IS.
BE EXTRA LOVING
IF YOU CAN.

You could be the sign or the inspiration someone

is looking for to know the simplicity of living with

lovingness. Don't keep your sweetness inside of you

or keep it exclusive to your inner circle. Let it be part

of how you move through the world. Be the person

cleo wade

who gives a dollar to someone in need on the street, waves at your neighbor, and smiles at a child walking by. We have all experienced instances in life where a loved one or even a stranger is sharp or harsh with us, and there is a part of us that feels compelled to react with the same energy. But we should ask ourselves: Why affirm negative energy when we can just as easily transform it into positive energy? <u>Be the reason someone realizes how simple it is to be nice.</u> Be someone's muse in that way. ❦

THE SPIRIT IS NEVER HOLDING
US BACK FROM AN
ATTITUDE ADJUSTMENT,
ONLY THE EGO DOES THAT.

cleo wade

With every new day and even every new minute, we have the opportunity to reset our attitude and change our perspective. There will always be people and circumstances that trigger our anger, sadness, or resentment, but when we allow those emotions to stay on a loop in our minds, that is on us, not on them. Instead, if we let go and allow the new day to bring new energy, we are given a clean slate to really understand what is upsetting us and problem-solve from a place of freshness rather than a place of hostility. When we have a better attitude, we create better solutions, and we have a better life. ⚘

RELEASE JUDGMENT. REPLACE IT
WITH LOVING KINDNESS. RELEASE
PRESSURE, REPLACE IT WITH CARE.
RELEASE COMPARISON,
REPLACE IT WITH GRATITUDE.

To reach our most divine potential, we must shed

what does not serve us and exchange it with what does.

Judgment does not feel good. It does not feel good to

be judged, nor does it feel good to judge others. When

we are feeling judged, we often react by responding

with judgment. There are two problems with this strategy. One, when we respond with judgment we lose the ability to peacefully resolve a situation. The other problem with the strategy of responding with judgment when we feel judged is that we lose the ability to access peace of mind. Judgmental thinking is negative thinking, and negative thinking usually triggers more negative thinking. Don't allow judgment to poison your positive thought flow. When our thought life is positive, our mind is calm, optimistic, and ready to powerfully problem-solve. ❦

Intimacy requires us to be careful with ourselves. *Full of care.* Intimacy with our thoughts means being careful with them and showing them affection when we have moments of insecurity or doubt, and by expressing our emotions rather than suppressing them. Intimacy with our body means taking care of our body by feeding it with life-affirming food, language, and movement rather than abusing it with shame, holding it to impossible standards, and weighing it down with toxic substances inside it. Intimacy with ourselves means showing up for all aspects of our being and doing it with trust, gentleness, and care. When

we learn how to have intimacy with ourselves, we

are much braver when it comes to creating intimacy

with others. ⋎

KNOWING IT WITHIN
HELPS US TO BE
BETTER AT HAVING
IT WITH OTHERS.

## with eyes closed

I hold myself tightly and say
I am in this with you
I am here for you
no matter what happens
I will take care of you

doing this
is me
choosing to be on my own team

doing this
is me
learning to hold myself down through even a
hurricane

doing this
is how I am able to
live my life
rather than let
my life
live me

*self-intimacy is self-care, self-care is self-love*

# rooting for each other

do you think
Mother Nature
cares
that any of her
beautiful flowers
grow in an array
of shades and sizes?
or that one grows
in this direction
and one grows in
that direction?
no,
she puts all of them in her
magnificent garden
so they may
be together
and
root
for
each
other

We are here to connect, not compare. There is a reason we are not in this world alone. It is because we are all connected and need each other to function peacefully, purposefully, and powerfully. We cannot know happiness or our true power if we are constantly in a state of comparison and competition. Comparison and extreme competition run on insecurities and the belief in scarcity, which inevitably isolates us from one another. Competition believes there is one pie, and when someone else takes a piece of it there is less for others. Our highest self knows that there is no pie.

Connection rejects the idea of competing for any one thing and runs, instead, on gratitude and abundance, which weave us more deeply into each other's lives so that we may better support each other in the world. Connection knows that everything we accomplish in life is much more fulfilling when we help others along the way. Don't let the spirit of comparison and competition take you somewhere fast, when the spirit of collaboration can take you some place far instead. ⋎

# what to do with what we learn

I did not come
into this room
to see the world
through your eyes
I cannot do that
I came here
to listen
not
merely
with my ears
but with
my heart
tell me your
story
and may
I leave
loving more
and knowing better
may I leave here
carrying you in my spirit
as I walk out of
this room
and into
another

cleo wade

No two people are the same, and no two people experience or process a situation the same way. Leave room for the other person's point of view. It matters. Our reality is not the only reality, and it is not wise for us to believe that our reality is the only correct one. We are not here to see things the same way. We are here to share ideas and be in community with each other, and we can only do that by respecting each other's perspectives so that we may cocreate a culture where everyone is better loved and kept safe. ⚘

LET LOVE BE THE
ANSWER TO ALL
OF LIFE'S QUESTIONS
(EVEN THE REALLY,
REALLY HARD ONES).

It takes so much bravery to let love be the answer

to all of the questions in our life, especially the dif-

ficult questions during the difficult times, but com-

mitting to that level of courageous tenderness is

exactly what is needed most in the face of adversity. When we decide that we are going to love no matter what, we embody the ability to make peace in a way that can transcend any struggle or conflict. Don't let any situation cause you to create blocks between you and your ability to give love and empathy. Be fearless enough to love without barriers. It is not always easy, but it is always worth it. Let the enduring strength of love carry you through whatever you encounter in life. This is what it means to truly live with compassion. ❦

OUR WISDOM DOES NOT JUST
COME FROM WHAT WE LEARN.
IT ALSO COMES FROM
WHAT WE UNLEARN.

cleo wade

$A$s we go through life, we begin to realize how much our experiences and environments are absorbed into our personality. For example, if we were raised in a home where people yelled when they were angry, then we are very likely to express ourselves the same way when we get angry, or accept that behavior from others. That said, it is never too late to decide to break our habits or change our behavior. When we empower ourselves to unlearn unhealthy behavior, we create more space to learn new and improved ways of being in the world. So whether you do it on your own or with the help of others, unlearn a little. It may teach you more than you could ever imagine. ❧

FEELING COMPLETE
ONLY COMES WITH
THE REALIZATION THAT
WE ARE ALL ONE.

cleo wade

It is so important to recognize that we are all one. You and your children are one. You and your neighbor are one. You and your partner are one. The dangers of the world are furthered only when we decide that the suffering of others is not our problem. Do not live your life in a bubble and, if you do, let it be one that is large enough for all of humanity. Understanding oneness is the first step to understanding inner peace, outer peace, and holistic happiness. ❦

## keep shooting for the moon

this may look
like a crash and burn
but it is just
gravity
in its beauty
asking
us to touch down
asking us
to feel the earth we come from
before we reach for the stars
again

# tired

I was tired of worrying
so I gave myself my peace back
I was tired of feeling intimidated by what I *should* do
so I pulled up my sleeves
and
got to work on what I *could* do
I was tired of not knowing
so I found out—about myself, my family, my
ancestors, my government, and the struggles of others
I was tired of seeing evil everywhere
so I found the heavenly spots and showed my
neighbors where they
were
I was tired
of looking at the world as one big mess
so I decided to
start cleaning it up
and when people ask me if I am exhausted
I tell them no
because
more than anything
what I got the most tired of
was being tired

Move beyond tolerance. We are not on this planet to tolerate each other. We are here to love each other. We are here to look out for each other. We are here to see each other reach our individual and collective potential. Tolerance is a low-level energy; it has no wings.

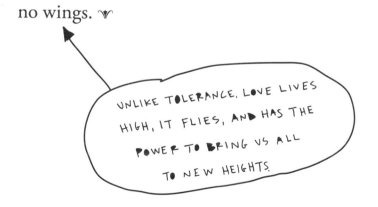

UNLIKE TOLERANCE, LOVE LIVES HIGH, IT FLIES, AND HAS THE POWER TO BRING US ALL TO NEW HEIGHTS.

cleo wade

CONFLICT IS INEVITABLE:
ENCOUNTERING CONFLICT
IN OUR LIVES DOES NOT
SAY ANYTHING ABOUT
WHO WE ARE, IT IS OUR
BEHAVIOR IN CONFLICT
THAT SAYS EVERYTHING
ABOUT WHO WE ARE.

Because there is no avoiding conflict in life, it is crucial that we learn to get good at disagreeing with each other. When we remember that not every difference in opinion is an attack, we are able to give the love, the respect, and the compassionate listening required to handle conflict peacefully. Just because someone disagrees with us does not mean that they are against us. Because conflict puts us in such a defensive place, it can trigger anger, frustration, and fear, which often makes us lash out, lose our temper, or shut down. When we realize that there is no such thing as a conflict-free life, we can instead choose to view every conflict as an opportunity to interact with others with a wider heart. Rather than letting conflict prompt behavior that we may not be particularly proud of, let it instead act as a trigger to dive more deeply into lovingkindness. The next time you find yourself in conflict, see it as an opportunity to show the power and bigness of your love. ❧

P.S. OUR IDEAS CAN CONFLICT WITHOUT US BEING IN CONFLICT.

DON'T BE THE REASON

SOMEONE

FEELS INSECURE.

BE THE REASON

SOMEONE

FEELS SEEN, HEARD,

AND SUPPORTED

BY THE

ENTIRE UNIVERSE.

cleo wade

The potential for our love to create a macro impact on the world is based on the amount of love we are able to put into our micro connections. Because all of our actions hold energy, everything we do has the power to affect another person. How do you treat others? How do you talk to people? Whether it is your best friend or a stranger, be someone who sees them, who affirms their dignity, and who honors their humanity. Be the person who gives someone the relief of knowing that the world ain't so bad after all. ♥

Oftentimes when the world feels chaotic, we begin to feel as if it is somehow inappropriate to have joy. Have your joy. Joy is a form of radical self-care. Joy energizes us to take on even the most difficult circumstances. When we have joy, especially in the midst of challenging times, we are saying to the world "I will define the current state of the world around me instead of allowing it to define me." Today, regardless of what is happening, empower yourself by embracing your joy. ❧

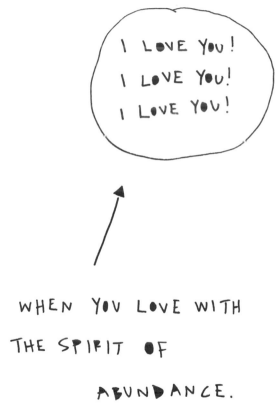

WHEN YOU LOVE WITH
THE SPIRIT OF
ABUNDANCE.

cleo wade

Our words are an extension of our energy. Our words also affirm our energy. If self-love is your struggle, say "I love you" to yourself every single day. It is a way we remind ourselves that we are dedicated to our relationship with ourselves. If you are looking to bring deeper connectivity to your relationships with others, let "I love you" be a declaration you frequently tell the people in your life. It feels good to say I love you. It feels good to let others know that you love them so they don't have to wonder. Affirming our feelings with our words is a way of actively and lovingly investing in the bond we have with ourselves and with everyone else. ❧

THE MOST POWERFUL THING

WE CAN DO WITH WHAT WE

CHOOSE IS TO REGULARLY

RE-CHOOSE IT.

cleo wade

Relationships run on rededication and recommitment. No relationship can sustain itself on one big gesture or one moment of shining behavior. Harmony and stability in our relationships with ourselves, our families, our friends, and our partners come from showing up every single day with a fresh desire for growth, intimacy, and goodness. Love cannot flourish on autopilot. It requires renewed devotion every moment of every day. Devote yourself to love. ᴡ

GRATITUDE IS A

CELEBRATION WE

ARE ALL INVITED TO.

I saw a sign in my hometown one day that said,

"Until further notice . . . celebrate everything." I have

always kept it in my heart as a daily mantra, because

it exemplifies the simplicity of gratitude. Oftentimes

we think gratitude is this big and complicated idea,

but gratitude is simple. It is a thank-you to every-thing and everyone allowing you to be in your story while it unfolds. Our stories may take twists and turns that create barriers between us and our grati-tude, but when we start by finding gratitude in small ways, we will begin to build the momentum we need to find gratitude in big ways. Creating a habit of gratitude also helps us to find it when we need it most. Allow there to be lightness in the journey of finding your gratitude, remembering that it's a party to which you are always invited. ☙

AND REMEMBER — LIFE IS

BIGGER THAN THE BOXES

WE CHECK ALONG THE WAY.

The world is constantly asking us to identify who

we are based on checking a box. We put so much

pressure on ourselves to live within whichever box

we are checking, but the most empowering thing

we could ever do with boxes is design our own. You

are not who you are because of which job, person-ality type, gender, or race box you check. You are who you are because you are not a box at all, and if you were a box, you would be one that is immense enough to hold all of the boxes that make you feel excited to be alive. So whether it is a writer, cook, accordion player, *New York Times* crossword-puzzle champ, parent, dog-walker, CEO, or lawyer . . . be all of the things. ❦

## being and becoming

be who you are
be who you want to be
make those
the same thing
arrive in the world
each day
embracing
yourself

# brave enough to show up

yell
if you need to

need
if you need to

live
while you
are here


The world does not need your silence. The world
does not need you to say you
are fine when you aren't.

EXPRESS YOURSELF. DON'T WALK
AROUND WITH THE BURDEN
OF UNSAID THINGS, UNLIVED
TALENTS, AND UNTOLD STORIES.
FREE YOURSELF. LIVE OUT LOUD.

cleo wade

You will never regret standing up for yourself or standing up for someone else. We always have the ability to use our light and our words to protect ourselves and our neighbors from harm. When we allow hurtful or negative behavior to pollute the environment around us, we do a disservice to everyone. No one deserves to be bullied, marginalized, or humiliated by others. Standing up for ourselves and others is something we can always be proud of. Do not allow for darkness to spread because of your silence. Shine light with your voice and your actions instead. ⋎

# the time has always been now

the time is always right
to begin
the time is always right
to stop waiting on you
the time is always right
to embrace your path
to accept what you had to walk through yesterday
and what you must step away from now as you move toward
tomorrow.
the time is always right
to pound your chest and let them know that you are here.
to let them know that they will hear you
to let them know that they will see you.
the time is always right to
end your silence.
to look at the person next to you and tell them to end their
    silence too
the time is always right to reclaim your narrative
to tell your story
to live with wild freedom
in a place that asks you to
control not only the way you see the world
but also
the way you see yourself
the time is always right to say

I will not be a victim
I will be a survivor
I will be a savior
the time is always right
to remind yourself that you
are going to be okay
the time is always right to love somebody
especially if that somebody is you
the time is always right
to make today
the day
you proclaim that you deserve
your ideas, your dreams, and your hopes
the time is always right
to let waiting
be something
you just don't
do anymore

now is the time,
beloved,
now is the time.

SURROUND YOURSELF

WITH PEOPLE WHO

DESERVE YOUR MAGIC.

One of the chief ways you show yourself love is by surrounding yourself with loving people. When you love yourself, you respect the sacred space you take up in the world. You recognize that no one who sucks your energy, puts you down, makes you feel small, or is unloving to you is entitled to your time. Look around you today and ask yourself if there is anyone in your life that is not showing you the good love you know you deserve. ❦

BEING WEIRD IS WHEN YOU
LOVE YOURSELF ENOUGH TO
LIBERATE YOURSELF FROM
THE BURDEN OF TRYING
TO BE NORMAL. IT IS ALSO
WHEN YOU ARE SMART ENOUGH
TO KNOW THAT THERE IS
NO SUCH THING AS NORMAL.

cleo wade

KNOW THAT YOU ARE VALUABLE.

KNOW THAT YOU ARE WORTHY.

KNOW THAT YOU ARE RARE.

HOW COULD ANYONE BE

BETTER THAN YOU IF

YOU ARE THE ONLY YOU?

* SAY THIS TO YOURSELF EVERY SINGLE DAY UNTIL
YOU BELIEVE IT. IT IS TRUE. IT IS REAL. YOU BELONG.

YOU BELONG YOU BELONG YOU BEL
BELONG YOU BELONG YOU BELONG
LONG YOU BELONG YOU BELONG YO
YOU BELONG YOU BELONG YOU BEL
BELONG YOU BELONG YOU BELONG
LONG YOU BELONG YOU BELONG
BELONG YOU BELONG YOU BELO
BELONG YOU BELONG YOU BELO
YOU BELONG YOU BELONG YOU
YOU BELONG YOU BELONG YO
LONG YOU BELONG YOU BELON
YOU BELONG YOU BELONG YOU BE
YOU BELONG YOU BELONG YOU BELO
YOU BELONG YOU BELONG YOU BE
BELONG YOU BELONG YOU BELO

s YOU BELONG YOU BELONG YOU
BELONG YOU BELONG YOU BE-
BELONG YOU BELONG YOU BELONG
G YOU BELONG YOU BELONG YOU
U BELONG YOU BELONG YOU BE-
U BELONG YOU BELONG YOU
YOU BELONG YOU BELONG YOU
- YOU BELONG YOU BELONG
ELONG YOU BELONG YOU BELONG
BELONG YOU BELONG YOU BE-
YOU BELONG YOU BELONG
JG YOU BELONG YOU BELONG
- YOU BELONG YOU BELONG
JG YOU BELONG YOU BELONG YOU
YOU BELONG YOU BELONG YOU BELONG

AND PERHAPS THAT ONE THING
THAT YOU HAVE SPENT YOUR
LIFE WORKING AROUND IS THE
ONE THING YOU ARE MEANT TO
WORK THROUGH INSTEAD.

What are you turning a blind eye to? What aspects of others do you ignore because "it's not even worth it"? What thoughts are you having that you have to talk yourself into feeling are "not that big of a deal"? What are you numbing? There are many circumstances, dynamics, and experiences in our lives that we bribe ourselves to work around, and sometimes that is okay. But it is worth it to ask yourself if any of the things you are working around are keeping you up at night or are things that you are constantly venting about to your friends. If so, change your strategy. Choose to work through what is upsetting you. Dissect it, get to know it, and if you need help, get help. Nothing negative deserves to take up major real estate in your mind or in your heart. ⸙

AND WHY NOT MAKE
ALL YOUR TALKS WITH
YOURSELF PEP TALKS?

cleo wade

You are the first person you speak to in the morning. What does that sound like? Are you trashtalking yourself *to* yourself? Are you celebrating yourself? Are you creating a nervous chatter? How you speak to yourself sets the tone for how the rest of the world will speak to you; use that power to lift yourself up and set a standard for loving communication. How you speak to yourself also sets the tone for how you will speak to others. If you learn how to lift yourself up with your words, you will be able to do the same for everyone else. Our world needs more cheerleaders. Start by being one for yourself.

## it's all beautiful

why should I
believe in
flaws?

because there is one way that we are all supposed to look?
because someone is selling me something to make me look
more like someone else?

so a company can profit off of not only my money but also my
self-esteem?

because as long as there is a standard of beauty, one type of
person can be celebrated while the rest of us are left out?

wanting, starving, shaming, and hating our beautiful bodies.

why should I
believe in
flaws?

whoever created the concept
does not believe in
me.

let us no longer "embrace our flaws"; we have none. I am me.
you are you.

it's all beautiful.

# a love note to my body

a love note to my body:

first of all,
I want to say
thank you.

for the heart you kept beating
even when it was broken

for every answer you gave me in my gut

for loving me back
even when I didn't know how to love you

for every time you recovered when I pushed you past our limits

for today,

for waking up.

# FYI: YOU ARE LOVABLE

When you express deep vulnerability or pain, you are still deserving of love. When you are embarrassed, you are still deserving of love. When you are angry, you are still deserving of love. When you need help, you are still deserving of love. When you have to try again, you are still deserving of love. When everything hurts, you are still deserving of love. When you make a mistake, you are still deserving of love. When you cry, you are still deserving of love. Don't let the opinions of others, the "rules" of society, or your own self-shaming uproot you from knowing that you are lovable. When you disconnect with your lovability, you disconnect with your ability to heal. No matter what happens, know that you are always deserving of love. ❧

## the day I came home and
## turned on the light

to those
who did not treat me well
and, for some reason, wondered why I left:

it is because
I remembered that
I loved myself more
than I loved the idea of
an
"us"

it is because
I remembered
I was worth more
than you could ever
give

it is because
I realized I did not need you

because
I had
me

*the day I came home and turned the light on*

AND MAY YOUR

FIRST LOVE

LAST FOREVER.


P.S. YOU ARE YOUR FIRST LOVE.

TAKE CARE OF YOURSELF.

## getting there

the mind says:
this river has no bottom
the heart says:
we can build a bridge here

I WISH I COULD GIVE YOU
ONE SOLUTION FOR PAIN
THAT DEFINITELY WORKS.
I CAN'T. IT IS A PROCESS
AND IT IS DIFFERENT
FOR EVERYONE, BUT WHAT
I CAN TELL YOU IS THAT
IF YOU ARE BADASS ENOUGH
TO FEEL YOUR PAIN, THEN
YOU ARE BADASS ENOUGH
TO HEAL YOUR PAIN.

LEAN INTO THE TOUGH STUFF.
GROWTH IS NOT ALWAYS
COMFORTABLE. THIS IS WHY
WE CALL THEM GROWING PAINS
NOT GROWING PLEASURES.

cleo wade

Very few breakthroughs come without a few breakdowns along the way. Stay the course. Our personal evolution brings so much brilliance to our life, but it can also bring some pain and discomfort with it. While our spiritual and emotional shifts do bring us closer to our best selves, they also simultaneously move us away from the space in which we may have been comfortably living before. These transitional periods, while necessary to our growth, often leave us feeling incredibly vulnerable. Be gentle with yourself. Moving from where you were to where you are takes some getting used to. ❦

HEARTS BREAK.

THAT'S HOW THE MAGIC GETS IN.

Heartbreak is so incredibly mysterious. While on the one hand, we are in so much pain with amplified feelings of loneliness and abandonment, we are also in such an elevated state of sensitivity, allowing us to be hugely in tune to the information our heart has to offer us. When we are in this state of intense intimacy with our heart, we are able to learn so many lessons that benefit our journey and future relationships. We can only fully tap into all that our emotional intelligence has to offer when we are able to really sit with what we are feeling, even when what we are feeling is pain. Try not to avoid pain too much. There is a certain type of magic that comes through pain, for it is where we learn of our power to keep going no matter what we go through. ☙

# what happens to pain

time and time again
my soul
and
my spirit
and
my learning heart
prove to me

*I heal*

# it gets better

you will not have the blues forever

forever
is the only thing that lasts forever

when the night sky
falls upon you
look up at her
see the darkness and the vastness
of her blues
hold your eyes steady on her
watch
the sun sneak in
see how even she, the great big sky,
changes with
the new day

*this too shall pass*

AND MAYBE I HAD BEEN SO
BUSY LOOKING FOR THE PIECES—
I NEVER NOTICED I WAS
ALREADY TOGETHER.

THE WAY YOU LOVE YOURSELF SETS THE

EXAMPLE FOR HOW EVERYONE ELSE

WILL LOVE YOU. SET THE BAR BY

SHOWING YOURSELF RESPECT, LOYALTY,

COMPASSION, KINDNESS, CARE, AND

VULNERABILITY. SHOW US ALL

HOW LOVING YOU IS DONE.

## reciprocity

what you want
must be held
in the same
hand
as what
you
give

cleo wade

The energy of reciprocity is what balances our relationships. Healthy reciprocity is not just about giving and receiving, it is about doing those two things well. When we attach exhaustion or resentment to the way we give, then we are not giving in a way that truly helps or benefits anyone involved. Giving should never feel like a negative experience. Equally, when we attach guilt or shame to receiving, we are blocking our ability to receive in a way that truly nourishes us. Our ability to give is only as powerful as our ability to receive, mostly because the more we can know how to receive, the more we have to give. 🌱

## love is an action verb

I loved back
not because
their love
sounded sweet
but because
their love
had feet
it did not
tell you where
it was going
it showed
you

cleo wade

We can accept only what someone has the ability to give us. When we are able to recognize the difference between someone's *desire* to do something and their *ability* to do something, we are much better at gauging our own expectations and needs from them. Our words often communicate what we *think* we are capable of, while our actions prove what we are *actually* capable of. You will have more clarity in your relationships when you accept the behavior of others based on their actions rather than on their words. ☙

FEAR WORRIES,
"HOW WILL I GET
THERE?"
FAITH SMILES
KNOWINGLY,
"WE WILL GET
THERE."

cleo wade

## forgiveness

do not
spend your time
trying to wrap your head
around
the idea of
forgiveness
it is not
intellectual

forgiveness

is spiritual
it is one of the most
spiritual things
we could ever do

Forgive yourself. Forgive yourself for who you were last week, last month, or last year. Forgive yourself for when you were exhausted and snapped at the people you love. Forgive yourself for not being able to do it all. Forgive yourself for your fears. Forgive yourself for your mistakes. Forgive yourself for eating one cookie too many. Forgive yourself for not being perfect. We often look at forgiveness as an intellectual act, but forgiveness is very spiritual. It is one of the most spiritual things we can do. When we forgive, we acknowledge that we are far bigger and greater than one individual

moment. When we forgive, we are saying to the

universe: I will not imprison myself or anyone else

with anger, shame, judgment, or resentment. Gift

yourself this freedom. ✌

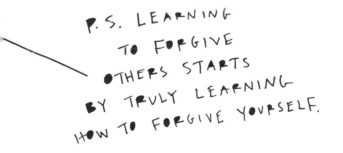

P.S. LEARNING TO FORGIVE OTHERS STARTS BY TRULY LEARNING HOW TO FORGIVE YOURSELF.

## strong flower

baby,
you are
the strongest
flower
that ever
grew
remember that
when
the weather
changes

Know that you are strong. Every living thing on this planet is here with the divine support of Mother Nature. She always has your back. Her type of support system will see you through any weather. The best thing about strength is that when you embody it, you further it, you get stronger. We grow into exactly where we need to be emotionally, spiritually, physically, and intellectually in a way that allows us to handle whatever life has in store for us. Knowing this keeps us inherently prepared so that we can enjoy the sun without worrying about the rain. 🌱

YOU ARE
IN BLOOM.
DID YOU
KNOW THAT?
YOU ARE

IN BLOOM
YOUR WHOLE
LIFE. DID
YOU KNOW
THAT TOO?

I THINK ABOUT
LOVE

(a poem)

I think about love
I wrote on a sheet of paper
one day
love, if you know how.
how to love?
a universe with
no road maps
no gravity
no luxury of polarity
up
feeling so
down

down
feeling
so
down

I think about how
we
want it all
to be
free

and to be
sheltered

to be
the home
and
be *in*
the home
at the same time

I think about
what it means
to be free
*in* love
to be free
*with* love

I think about
having the clarity
to know
when to stay
and
when
to go

have we not all
at one point
stayed too long?

cleo wade

I think about
staying too long
it
reminds me
of
past loves

ghosts

as you love
you learn
of ghosts
you are not haunted
by
the person
but
by all
of the ways
you wish
you would have been

the ways
you wish
you knew how
to be

growing up
they do not teach you
all the things
of love

they tell you
love hurts
but
they never tell you
that
there are
some people
there are
some things
you never
get over

I think about
heartbreak
how
hearts break
and
that's how
the magic
gets in

the magic
by the way
does
get in
it never stops
getting
in
but
the other thing
no one tells you
when
you are young
is that
hearts
do not
unbreak
they remain

in pieces
and with
these pieces
you go on
and
you go on

until
one day
you meet
someone
who has pieces too
and together

you
make
a new heart

the other thing
no one tells you
when
you are young
is that
you
meet the person
who
helps you
make
a new heart

and
it is

cleo wade

a gift of
grace and
beauty

beyond imagination

I think about
the gift
of love

how we struggle
to
understand how
to
receive
such a gift

rumi said:
"your task
is not
to seek
for love
but merely
to seek
and find
all of the barriers

within yourself
you have
built up against it"

I think about
how
we should
get to know ourselves
without barriers

I think about
how
we should
get to know ourselves
in a state
that
is not seeking

I think about
how
we are all
chasing
our dreams
meanwhile
our dreams
are

chasing
us

I think about
dreams when
I think about
love
for
one does not exist
without
the other
as
the inhale
is to
the exhale

I think
you should
have good love

I think
you should
have your dreams

I think
those things

belong to you
who else
could they
possibly
belong to
more than you?
and yes
you may
have to
fight for them

that
I know
for sure

and yes
the biggest
battle
may be with
yourself
and
on your own behalf
there is a lot of love
in
our battles

cleo wade

for
to live your life
as a soldier
fighting every day
for
who the hell you are
is
a very strong life

be proud of that

when I think about
being proud

I think about
where
I am from
and
when I say
where
I am from

I mean

a woman

as a girl
I was not sure
how to be

I said things
I did not mean

I said things
I did not
understand

as
a woman
I still have
moments
of being
outside of myself
but
as
a woman
I know now
to ask
what they mean
to
try to understand

cleo wade

to
not only be the help
I need but
to
ask for it
as well

I think about
needing
how
a strange shame
comes
from needing another

how
what's worse
is
the way
we try
to not need
anything from
ourselves

how we
do not ask
what

we need
so
instead
wonder
who
we are

do not
wonder who you are
*find out* who you are

remembering

that
to decide
to
really and
truly
get to know yourself
is
the bravest
thing
you
could ever do

*decide on you*

cleo wade

be
the moon
if you want to

be
the lightbulb
in the kitchen
or a flashlight
in the wild

all
I ask
is that
you
shine

for

how to love
can be
a dark universe
with
no signals
where
the lessons
only come

when the past
is
the past
and
you are
sharing your
ghost stories
with
your new heart


but the more
I think about it
the more
I see

that
the clearest route
to bliss
is to
be
alive
while
you
are here
to

be
with yourself
in a
love
so deep
the oceans
get jealous and
even
outer space
wants
to
be inside

that

is
the type
of love
that
shows us all
how

that

is the starting point
from which

to
build
a home
you can invite

the
whole world
into

cleo wade

# acknowledgments

I would first like to acknowledge my ancestors and all that came before me. There would be no space in the world for me if they had not first dreamt it and fought for it.

To my brother, Bernardo, who continuously shows me the unbreakable nature of the human spirit and the power within us all to change.

To my mother, Lori, for teaching me what unconditional love and true forgiveness means.

To my father, Bernardo, for teaching me resilience and the art of celebrating life and love.

To Cory, for being a constant source of light and inspiration in my life. You have truly been my rock during this process. Thank you, ML.

To Jewels Rosaasen for keeping me sane; I treasure you beyond words.

To Jenna Barclay, who spent countless hours workshopping this book with me. I am eternally grateful for the many ways you have nurtured my spiritual journey over the years.

To Heather Karpas for your passion, incredible friendship, and dedication to this book.

To Dawn Davis, Dana Sloan, Trisha Tan, Albert Tang, and the entire team at 37 INK, this book would not be possible without your hard work. Thank you one million times.

A special thank-you to all of the Goddesses, Queens, Soul Sisters, and Angels in my life. You are my muses, my support system, and my family. I would not be the woman I am without the love, magic, and friendship we share.

These pages have been inspired by many friends and mentors along the way. Thank you all for your advice and wisdom.

And to everyone who has supported my work over the years, thank you for being a part of my family. You mean the world to me.

Love,

Cleo

An adaptation
of the animated film
*Raggedy Ann & Andy—
A Musical Adventure*

THE BOBBS-MERRILL COMPANY, INC.

Indianapolis / New York

by

KATHLEEN N. DALY

based on the screenplay by

PATRICIA THACKRAY and MAX WILK

*Based on the Original Stories and Characters
Created by Johnny Gruelle*

*Raggedy Ann and Raggedy Andy and all related characters
appearing in this book are trademarks of The Bobbs-Merrill
Company, Inc.*

Published by The Bobbs-Merrill Company, Inc.
Indianapolis   New York

ISBN 0-672-52301-9
Library of Congress catalog card number 76-47894
Manufactured in the United States of America

First printing

# Contents

# Marcella's Playroom

MARCELLA JUMPED off the school bus in even more of a hurry than usual. In one hand she carried her lunch box. In the other she carried a rag doll.

"It's my birthday, my birthday!" she cried happily, giving the rag doll a shake.

She set off at a trot, her feet scuffling through the crisp autumn leaves that lay along the sidewalk and in the gutters. The late afternoon sunlight filtered through the red-gold leaves on the branches and glinted on her long, shining hair.

The rag doll wore a happy smile, even though she *was* being carried by one foot and her head was trailing in the leaves.

Raggedy Ann was always happy, you see, because she had a sweet smile stitched upon her face. And inside her soft, cotton-stuffed body beat a little heart of candy. Anybody who has a candy heart thinks sweet thoughts and spreads love and sunshine all around.

But still, she did wish that Marcella would be a little more careful. Bumpety-bumpety-bump went her head as Marcella bounded up the porch steps.

"Marcella, is that you?" called her mother from the kitchen.

"It's me, it's me!" cried Marcella.

"Hurry up and get ready, dear. It's almost time for your party."

"Yes, Mother," called Marcella.

She flung open the door of her playroom.

"Hello, Susie. Hello, Grandpa. Hello, all you dollies! I hope you haven't been naughty while I've been away."

She climbed up to the bookshelf and picked up a

12

heavy glass ball. "Hello, Captain, how's your snowstorm today?" As she shook the ball, the "snow" whirled around the little figure of the Captain and his ship.

"Come on, dear," called Marcella's mother.

Marcella put Raggedy Ann gently on a chair.

"Now Raggedy Ann, you take care of all the others while I'm gone," she said.

Then she skipped out of the playroom and closed the door with a slam.

For a moment all was quiet inside the playroom. And then something very strange began to happen. One by one the dolls began to move and sigh and yawn and stretch. Yes, they were coming to life, just as they did every time they were left to themselves, with no real-for-sure people around.

"Grandpa, is that door truly closed?" asked Raggedy Ann.

Grandpa Doll trotted over to the door and checked.

"Yes, Annie, the coast is clear, all right."

Raggedy Ann gave a deep sigh.

"Goodness, what a day I've had. Bumpety-bump, bumpety-bump all day. It's always like that when she's excited about something." She felt her head. "I think I must have popped some of my stitches."

"Never mind," said Maxi, trundling over on his wheel. "Maxi will fix your head. Maxi Fix-It, that's me!"

"I'll help you, too," said Susan, the plump Pincushion Doll.

Together they neatened up Raggedy Ann's head.

"There, that's better," said Raggedy Ann. "Thank you."

"The way you go bouncing around with Marcella, it's a wonder you haven't lost all your stuffing," said Susan disapprovingly.

Raggedy Ann laughed. "Oh, but I have. Many's the

13

time I've come unstuffed and been restuffed and sewn and sewn. I was around long before Marcella, you know. I sat in a box in the attic for fifty years before she found me!"

Nobody could quite imagine what fifty years must be like, so they all stayed quiet for a minute.

"Still, you do get to see the world outside," said Grandpa.

"Yes, the world outside," said the Twin Penny Dolls, who always talked at the same time and said the same things. "Where do you go? What do you see? Do tell! Do tell!"

The dolls never tired of hearing Raggedy Ann tell of the outside world. They gathered around her.

"Well," said Raggedy Ann, "there are so many things—so many beautiful things."

"For instance?" said Maxi.

"There are beautiful butterflies fluttering by. There are leaves, and birds that sing. There are pretty flowers, with bees buzzing around them. And there are lots of people and children and puppies, smiling and happy."

"Is it really like that?" asked Grandpa, holding on to his corncob pipe.

"Yes, it really is," said Raggedy Ann, with her sweet smile.

"Annie, you always make everything seem beautiful and happy," said Susan.

"Things *are* beautiful," said Raggedy Ann. "But here's the best news of all—it's Marcella's birthday! She's seven years old today."

"Uh—what's a birthday?" asked Barney the Beanbag Doll.

"Well, it's a kind of thing that real-for-sure people have every year. They get older, one year at a time."

"And when the year's up, that's your birthday," said Grandpa. "You have parties and fun—and presents! Look over there!"

"*That* certainly looks like a present," said Susan.

"It just came, it just came!" chorused the Twin Dolls.

Raggedy Ann peered hard at the box. What were those strange things sticking out underneath? My, but they did look familiar. They looked sort of like her own feet. She stared down at her striped cotton socks and black cotton feet. Then she looked back at the box. Those things looked like—

"Andy!" she screamed. "Is that you?"

The feet wiggled frantically and there was a muffled groan.

HAPPY BIRTHDAY: Marcella
from Paris, France
CONTENTS: one French Doll
XXX Love from Aunt Sophie.

"Oh, dear," said Raggedy Ann. "Poor Andy is under there, all squashed. Please, everybody, let's push."

All the dolls gathered around and pushed and heaved. Gradually they got the box over to one side. Raggedy Andy, flat as a pancake, tried to move his wobbly legs.

"Gosh, what a relief!" he said faintly. Everybody helped him up. Susan got busy with her pins.

"Oh, poor Andy," said Raggedy Ann. "I hope it didn't hurt too much."

"Oh, no, not too much," said Raggedy Andy bravely. "Just give me a shake or two and I'll be as right as rain." Like his sister, Raggedy Ann, he could never stay cross for very long.

"Still, it was no fun being under that box all day," muttered Raggedy Andy. "I wonder what's in it."

"There's a label on it, up there, but I can't read it from here," said Raggedy Ann. "Boost me up."

Raggedy Andy, Grandpa, Barney the Beanbag Doll, The Sockworm, Topsy, the Twin Dolls—all the dolls got together in an untidy heap. There was so much giggling and heaving that the heap kept falling apart, but at last Raggedy Ann made her way to the top and grabbed the label.

"It says, 'Happy Birthday, Marcella, from Paris, France.

Contents: One French Doll. Love from Aunt Sophie.'"

"Ooh!" gasped the Twin Dolls. "Imagine that!"

"A doll all the way from Paris, France!" exclaimed Maxi.

"Another doll," groaned Raggedy Andy, quite unlike his usual cheery self. Marcella would have been surprised to see that his mouth was pulled down at the corners. "That's all we need—another doll. A *girl* doll, all sugar and spice, I bet."

"Andrew, you're just terrible," said Raggedy Ann. "It must be because of being squashed all day."

"Anyone would feel the same," said Grandpa sympathetically. "Who wants to be squashed all day—even by a French doll?"

Maxi grinned. "I wouldn't mind."

Suddenly Grandpa was waving his arms up and down. "Freeze!" he said. "Here comes Marcella!"

Quickly the dolls hurried back to where Marcella had left them. All except Raggedy Andy, who flopped down just beside the box, smiling sweetly.

# The
# French Doll

THE DOOR to the playroom flew open, and in came Marcella. Her cheeks were flushed and rosy. She wore a silver paper crown.

"Oh, Raggedies, what a lovely party I'm having! But I couldn't wait one more minute to come up and see my surprise. It's from Paris, France!"

She slipped the string off the box and ripped open the brown paper. There were oceans of pink tissue paper, crinkling and rustling. Finally Marcella pulled out a doll. But this was no ordinary doll.

"Ooh!" gasped Marcella. "A French doll!"

The doll was very beautiful. She had painted cheeks and a little rosebud mouth. Her hair was blond and tightly curled. Her eyes were shiny blue, fringed with long, dark eyelashes.

Marcella stroked the soft hair and smoothed out the long skirt and petticoats.

"What shall I call you?" she wondered aloud. She tipped up the doll to look at the pretty white underwear.

"Ba-bette . . . Ba-bette," said the doll's little mechanical voice.

20

"Babette," breathed Marcella. "How lovely. Look, dollies, here is a new friend for you. Look, Raggedy Ann, isn't she the most gorgeous, beautiful doll you ever saw in your whole life?"

Raggedy Ann smiled sweetly.

"You poor dear," said Marcella to Babette. "You've had such a long trip, all the way from Paris. You must be tired. I'm going to put you to bed in the dollhouse."

The dollhouse was very quaint and old-fashioned. It had been in Marcella's family for many years. It had a slanting roof and dormer windows. There were blue shutters that opened and closed.

Marcella opened up the hinged roof.

"This will be your house, Babette," said Marcella.

She put Babette in the biggest bedroom.

"Marcella! Come on down and blow out your birthday candles!"

"Coming, Mother," Marcella called downstairs. "Now, Babette, you settle down and rest. And you, Raggedy Ann, *dear* Raggedy Ann, make sure that Babette feels right at home every minute. She's a stranger here, and you and all the other dolls must be especially nice to her. See you soon!"

Marcella blew them all an airy kiss and skidded out the playroom door, which closed with a bang.

There was a moment's silence while the dolls made sure that Marcella was on her way.

Raggedy Ann was the first to stir. She untwined her legs and walked over to the dollhouse.

"Welcome to the playroom, Babette," she said softly.

There was no answer from the dollhouse.

"Babette?"

Raggedy Ann knocked on the door.

21

Raggedy Andy gave it a big thump, cupped his hands, and yelled, "Babette!"

The little blue door on the balcony opened and Babette came out, blinking sleepily.

"What is it? Who are you? What is this place?"

"My name is Raggedy Ann," beamed the little doll. "And this is my raggedy brother, Andy. Welcome, Babette!"

Babette blinked again, so that the long eyelashes fluttered.

"But where am I?" she asked.

"You're in the playroom, that's where," said Raggedy Andy. "Lots of dressing up and tea parties and things like that—*you'll* probably love it." He rubbed his elbow that was still a little out of shape from having been squashed all day.

Raggedy Ann gave him a look from one of her bright shoe-button eyes. "Now, Andy, we're supposed to be nice and make her feel welcome, remember?"

"Oh, dear," said Babette, "I have never been in a place like this. I come from the most expensive toyshop in Paris. You all look so—different."

"Never mind," said Raggedy Ann kindly. "You'll love it here with us."

"But—what exactly are you?" asked Babette. "I have never seen things like you before. In the toyshop, all the dolls had beautiful clothes and shiny faces and curly hair . . ."

"We are dolls, too," said Raggedy Ann. "Each of us is different on the outside. Some fat, some thin, some floppy, like Andy and me. But, you know, Babette, it doesn't matter what you look like outside, so long as you are beautiful inside."

# Captain Contagious

SUDDENLY there was a loud "A-choo!"

It was the Captain in the glass ball. He felt a little out of things, up there on the bookshelf.

"What's going on?" he asked his parrot Queasy. "Can't see a thing in here with all this blasted snow. Bring me my spyglass."

Babette didn't even hear him. She shook her head sadly. "I don't understand," she said. "This is so different from Paris. I wish I were home again."

"But this is your home now," said Raggedy Andy. "Why, Raggedy Ann is the sweetest, kindest doll in all the world. She will love you with all her loving candy heart. And so will we all—you wait and see."

Babette sighed and shook her head. Just as the Captain focused his spyglass upon her, a tiny, starry tear trickled from one blue eye.

"Shiver my timbers," said the Captain, his moustaches twirling. "What a beautiful doll! She's like a dream come true. I think she is my one and only true love, finally come right here to the playroom!"

Babette didn't hear him. She sighed again and turned to go into the house.

"I think she's a little homesick," said Raggedy Ann. "Poor thing. Perhaps she'll feel better after a good night's sleep."

The little blue door closed behind Babette.

"Queasy," yelled the Captain, "we must get out of here. A-a-choo!"

"Aye, aye, Captain," squawked the parrot. He had his eye on the Cuckoo Clock. It hung on the wall right near the Captain's shelf. And the hands of the clock were just moving up to the hour—five o'clock.

25

Quickly Queasy scratched the letters SOS, which meant HELP! on the glass inside the ball. The Captain's long whiskers curled around the letters.

At exactly five o'clock the yellow wooden doors of the Cuckoo Clock sprang open.

"Cuckoo-cuckoo-cuckoo-cuckoo-cuckoo!" screamed the Cuckoo. He knew his job all right, and he was proud of it. One "cuckoo" for every hour of the day.

On the fifth "cuckoo" he suddenly noticed the Captain, waving wildly. He saw the message scribbled on the glass wall.

"Oh, my," he said, which is very unusual for a Cuckoo Clock.

All the dolls looked up in amazement.

The Cuckoo came zooming down on his spring. He grabbed Raggedy Ann's yarn hair in his beak and sprang back, and Raggedy Ann landed on the shelf beside the glass ball.

"What is it? What's the matter?" asked Raggedy Ann.

Then she saw the Captain jumping up and down in clouds of snow. She saw the HELP message scribbled on the glass.

"Oh, my goodness," she said. "The Captain needs help. I'll do my best, Captain," she said. "Put me down, please, Cuckoo."

The Cuckoo dropped her as gently as he could, and Raggedy Ann landed with a *plop* on the playroom floor.

"Are you all right? Are you all right?" asked the Twin Dolls.

"Oh, yes," said Raggedy Ann, smiling. "We Raggedies don't have anything to break, you know. It's the Captain who needs our help. I think he wants to get out."

They all gazed up at the Captain, who was prancing up

and down, his long moustaches twirling, yelling things that they couldn't hear.

"You're right," said Raggedy Andy. "What are we going to do?"

"I must think," said Raggedy Ann.

She sat down in a heap and pulled her rag face down into a frown. Thinking was always difficult.

"Be careful, dear," said Susan, ready with her pins. Thinking always made Raggedy Ann's stitches come loose.

"I know!" said Raggedy Ann. "Maxi, look in your tool-box. Maybe you have a tool that can cut glass."

"I'll look," said Maxi. He took off his hat and felt inside his head. "Aha—the very thing!"

He drew out a very sharp-looking tool. "It's a glass cutter—for cutting glass," he said proudly.

"Oh, you are wonderful, Maxi," said Raggedy Ann. "Let's try it. Up, please, Mister Cuckoo Bird."

The Cuckoo hadn't had so much fun in years. He zoomed down again and grabbed Raggedy Ann's yarn hair. Maxi clung to her waist, and up they went.

"Now stand back, please," said Maxi.

Carefully he cut a circle in the glass. He tapped it gently with a hammer.

Suddenly a perfect circle of glass fell out of the ball.

"Look out!" yelled Maxi.

Nobody expected what happened next.

# Kidnapped!

WATER CAME gushing out of the hole, and with it came the Captain, his ship, his spyglass, and Queasy, squawking loudly for all to hear.

Everyone got very wet indeed, all except the Cuckoo. He sprang hastily back into the safety of his clock.

"Free at last!" cried the Captain. "Now I can claim that beautiful doll!"

Sea water sloshed over the playroom floor. All the dolls found themselves floating and gasping in the salty water. Most surprising of all, the Captain's ship got bigger and bigger.

"Avast! Belay!" He yelled all the nautical words he knew, and some of them were very naughty. His ship, which had been so tiny in its glass ball, was suddenly a splendid three-masted galleon, with a full crew of sailors. In fact, they were not only sailors, they were Pirates, with long black whiskers and striped jerseys, and each had a patch over one eye. They wore boots and carried wicked-looking cutlasses.

"Dear me, Captain," said Raggedy Ann, who was floating face up in the salty water. "What on earth are you doing?"

"Lay back there, Missy!" yelled the Captain. "I have come to claim my prize!"

"What prize?" gurgled Raggedy Andy, hoping desperately that his cotton stuffing wouldn't get soaked and send him to the bottom.

"My treasure! The beautiful Babette! A-choo!"

"Oh, dear," said Raggedy Ann, "I'm afraid you're going to catch a cold instead."

"Queasy, dowse the lights!" yelled the Captain.

Queasy flew up to the light and pulled the string. Suddenly there was darkness in the playroom.

The Captain made a rope out of his long whiskers and climbed up to Babette's balcony. A door smashed open. Babette shrieked. Then, kicking and screaming, she was carried out by the Captain. He brought her aboard his ship while the Pirates sang, "Yo ho for the life of a Pirate!"

"They are very naughty indeed," sighed Raggedy Ann, her little candy heart beating fast. "I don't know what's to become of them."

"Pull, me hearties!" cried the Captain. "Away we go!"

And away they went, the Pirates pulling lustily upon their oars, across the playroom floor, out the window, and into the night.

"Oh, how naughty," said Raggedy Ann. Still, she couldn't help admiring the song of the wicked Pirates as it faded into the distance.

"Yo ho, yo ho for the life of a Pirate!" they sang. "Trim the mizzen and shiver the timbers and hoist the main, yo ho!"

"The life of a Pirate is the only life for me!" joined in the Captain.

"*Eeeeek!*" screamed Babette.

"It's all my fault," said Raggedy Ann. "I should never have let him out."

The salty water had all disappeared with the wicked Captain and his crew. The dolls were shaking themselves and spluttering.

"Andy, I've got to save Babette!" said Raggedy Ann.

"You're not going after her?" said Grandpa, feeling slightly stiff after his soaking.

"Not into the Deep Deep Woods!" said Susan.

"It's really scary, really scary in the Deep Deep Woods," said the Twin Dolls, holding on to each other.

"I don't care how scary it is," said Raggedy Ann. "I've got to get Babette back for Marcella. It's her birthday doll."

"You're right," said Raggedy Andy. "I'm coming with you. After all, somebody's got to protect you."

The two Raggedies walked over to the windowsill and climbed up.

33

Raggedy Ann stood on the windowsill and looked down at all the little faces. "Now you stay here and wait. We'll be back before morning—just wait and see."

"And Marcella won't even know anything happened," added Raggedy Andy, sounding much braver than he felt. "I'll go first." He peered down into the darkness.

"No, I will," said Raggedy Ann. "It was all my fault."

"Ooh, ooh!" gasped the Twin Dolls as Raggedy Ann dropped out of the window.

"Now me," said Raggedy Andy. He gave a couple of little jumps to give himself courage. Before he knew it he was over the edge.

"Are you all right, Annie?" he gasped, trying to untangle his feet.

He helped Raggedy Ann up.

"I'm all right—I think," said Raggedy Ann. "How about you, Andy?"

"Oh, sure, of course," said Raggedy Andy.

They straightened themselves out, holding on to each other. The window of the playroom seemed awfully far above them. Ahead loomed the dark shadows of the Deep Deep Woods.

Where anything can happen.

35

# The Camel
# with the
# Wrinkled Knees

"ARE YOU afraid, Andy?" asked Raggedy Ann.

"Me, scared?" said Raggedy Andy. "Why should I be scared?"

"It is a *little* scary," said Raggedy Ann. "Ooh—what's that?"

"It's only an old hoot owl," said Raggedy Andy, clutching Raggedy Ann tightly. "Don't be afraid. I'll take care of you."

"You are brave, Andy," said Raggedy Ann.

"It's easy to be brave when we're together," said Raggedy Andy. "Besides, I've got this paper daisy you gave me once, the time I got washed and starched by mistake, remember?"

Raggedy Ann giggled. "Yes, and you were too stiff to move for weeks."

"Well, your paper flower cheered me up, and I've been carrying it around ever since."

"Oh, Andy, it's great that we've got each other."

Suddenly Raggedy Ann stopped and held her breath.

"What's that, Andy?" she whispered.

"What's what?" said Raggedy Andy.

A funny, whistling sound came from the darkness of the Deep Deep Woods.

"Oh, that," said Raggedy Andy. His raggedy knees were shaking just the tiniest little bit, but he put a firm arm around Raggedy Ann's shoulders.

"Don't worry, Annie. Whatever it is, I'll protect you."

Sigh, groan, snuffle . . . the sounds were coming nearer.

"Here it comes," whispered Raggedy Ann. The bushes ahead of them rustled, and a large head poked out.

"Come on out, whoever you are," said Raggedy Andy.

The head looked at them for a moment. Then out came the rest of the creature. It was a camel. But such a camel as you never saw in any zoo. He was made of soft woolen cloth and stuffed with sawdust. At one time he may have been a very handsome, important-looking camel. But

37

he had been played with so much that now he had
where no self-respecting camel is supposed to have it
And his legs, instead of being straight and stiff, were
wrinkly and baggy at the knees. When he moved, it seem
as if he would pitch forward at every step. And he was *bl*

Raggedy Andy took one astonished look, then leaped
forward and flung his arms around the Camel's neck.

"Got you!" he cried bravely.

The Camel's knees sagged more than ever, and he fell
in a crumpled heap, giving a great, squashy kind of groan.

"Andy, he's just a poor old camel," said Raggedy Ann,
rushing forward. "Let him go!"

"Oh, dearie me," groaned the Camel with the Wrinkled
Knees. "I'm afraid my legs aren't quite what they used to be.
Once they had good, straight sticks inside them. You should
have seen me then."

"Oh, poor, dear Camel," said Raggedy Ann. "Here, let
me help you up."

# The Camel
# with the
# Wrinkled Knees

"ARE YOU afraid, Andy?" asked Raggedy Ann.

"Me, scared?" said Raggedy Andy. "Why should I be scared?"

"It is a *little* scary," said Raggedy Ann. "Ooh—what's that?"

"It's only an old hoot owl," said Raggedy Andy, clutching Raggedy Ann tightly. "Don't be afraid. I'll take care of you."

"You are brave, Andy," said Raggedy Ann.

"It's easy to be brave when we're together," said Raggedy Andy. "Besides, I've got this paper daisy you gave me once, the time I got washed and starched by mistake, remember?"

Raggedy Ann giggled. "Yes, and you were too stiff to move for weeks."

"Well, your paper flower cheered me up, and I've been carrying it around ever since."

"Oh, Andy, it's great that we've got each other."

Suddenly Raggedy Ann stopped and held her breath.

"What's that, Andy?" she whispered.

"What's what?" said Raggedy Andy.

A funny, whistling sound came from the darkness of the Deep Deep Woods.

"Oh, that," said Raggedy Andy. His raggedy knees were shaking just the tiniest little bit, but he put a firm arm around Raggedy Ann's shoulders.

"Don't worry, Annie. Whatever it is, I'll protect you."

Sigh, groan, snuffle . . . the sounds were coming nearer.

"Here it comes," whispered Raggedy Ann. The bushes ahead of them rustled, and a large head poked out.

"Come on out, whoever you are," said Raggedy Andy.

The head looked at them for a moment. Then out came the rest of the creature. It was a camel. But such a camel as you never saw in any zoo. He was made of soft woolen cloth and stuffed with sawdust. At one time he may have been a very handsome, important-looking camel. But he had been played with so much that now he had lumps where no self-respecting camel is supposed to have lumps. And his legs, instead of being straight and stiff, were all wrinkly and baggy at the knees. When he moved, it seemed as if he would pitch forward at every step. And he was *blue*.

Raggedy Andy took one astonished look, then leaped forward and flung his arms around the Camel's neck.

"Got you!" he cried bravely.

The Camel's knees sagged more than ever, and he fell in a crumpled heap, giving a great, squashy kind of groan.

"Andy, he's just a poor old camel," said Raggedy Ann, rushing forward. "Let him go!"

"Oh, dearie me," groaned the Camel with the Wrinkled Knees. "I'm afraid my legs aren't quite what they used to be. Once they had good, straight sticks inside them. You should have seen me then."

"Oh, poor, dear Camel," said Raggedy Ann. "Here, let me help you up."

Together Raggedy Ann and Raggedy Andy heaved and pushed. At last the Camel with the Wrinkled Knees was standing almost upright.

"Thank you, thank you, much obliged," he said. He lifted his long, wrinkled neck and gazed up into the sky. "It's too bad you tripped me up. Now they have gone," he said.

"Gone?" said Raggedy Andy. "Who have gone?"

"Those lovely camels in the sky—a whole caravan of them, with nice straight legs and graceful necks, and all looking so happy and smiling . . ."

"Are you *sure?*" asked Raggedy Ann. She and Raggedy Andy were both staring up at the sky, but all they could see were the stars twinkling through the branches of the trees.

"Oh, yes," sighed the Camel with the Wrinkled Knees. "I often see them. I've been chasing them for ages. If only I could catch up with them, think how happy I'd be. I wouldn't be sad and alone anymore. I'd have friends who

would love me. They'd smooth out all my wrinkles, and I wouldn't be low-down saggy and raggy-baggy blue." He heaved such a deep sigh that Raggedy Ann was afraid he would fall over again.

"Oh, poor, dear Camel," she said, holding him up with her little shoulder. "Please, please, don't be sad. Andy and I will be your friends, won't we, Andy?"

"Oh, yes," said Raggedy Andy. "We'll be really-truly friends, and you'll see—everything will get better. Why, Annie here has the kindest heart in the world. It's a sugar-candy heart and it says on it, 'I love you.' *Everyone* is happy when Annie is around."

"My," said the Camel with the Wrinkled Knees, "that *does* sound nice. To have real friends. Are you sure?"

"Of course we're sure," said Raggedy Ann and Raggedy Andy together.

Suddenly the Camel with the Wrinkled Knees sagged again. Raggedy Ann and Raggedy Andy heaved him up.

"I can never be sure of anything," he moaned. "That's why I'm always chasing those camels in the sky. Look, look, there they are again!"

He started to move forward, pitching and swaying. "Quickly, come with me, or we'll lose them again!"

Raggedy Ann and Raggedy Andy looked up at the blue night sky. Then they looked at each other.

"I don't see anything, Andy, do you?"

"No," whispered Raggedy Andy. "This is really weird. Look at him go! We'd better hop aboard."

Nimbly they sprang onto the Camel's back, holding on very tight as the lumpy creature sagged and swayed, going faster and faster, his eyes on the sky.

"Mister Camel, please slow down," begged Raggedy Ann. "There are no camels up there!"

41

"There's happiness up there," said the Camel with the Wrinkled Knees. "I've been looking for happiness all my life. Can't let it get away from me now."

"Whoa, whoa!" yelled Raggedy Andy.

They were starting to climb a very steep hillside.

"Please be careful!" cried Raggedy Ann. "We're going too fast, and we don't know what's on the other side of the hill. Oh, please, Mister Camel . . ."

But it was too late. They had reached the top of the hill and had gone clean over the edge. They were falling through the air, arms and legs flying, going down, down . . .

# The Greedy

THE THREE—Raggedy Ann, Raggedy Andy, and the Camel with the Wrinkled Knees—slid down a slippery slope, their arms and legs all tangled up together.

They came to a slurpy, slithery, gooey stop at the bottom.

The Camel with the Wrinkled Knees groaned.

But Raggedy Andy, smelling something familiar, put out his hand and took up a dab of the sticky stuff.

He tasted it.

"It's taffy!" he said. "Really delicious taffy. Taste it, Annie."

"Yum," said Raggedy Ann. "It's almost as good as that taffy we made one night in the kitchen back home; do you remember, Andy?"

"Oh, yes," said Raggedy Andy. "What a lovely mess we made!"

"But we did clean it up," said Raggedy Ann. "It looks to me as if no one has done any cleaning up around here for a long time. Look at that—a giant cherry."

She reached over to pull the cherry out of the sea of taffy—and it started to move!

In fact, it started to grow.

In fact, "it" was alive.

"Urp," it gurgled. "Oh, excuse me. Pardon me. Who are you?" It looked at the two little dolls and the Camel with the Wrinkled Knees, who was sagging more than ever in the sweet, sticky stuff.

"Who are *you?*" said Raggedy Andy.

"I am the Greedy. And this is the Taffy Pit. Welcome to my home."

"What sort of a place is this?" asked Raggedy Andy, as a chocolate cupcake went sailing by.

"It's the sweetest place in the world," said the Greedy, rolling his eyes. "I've gathered sweets—every kind of sweet you ever thought of—from all over the place. They are all here. But I can never get enough to eat. Never, ever."

"Oh, dear," said Raggedy Ann. "That's terrible. Is there anything we can do to help?"

"Yes," burped the Greedy. "Excuse me. If you could only tell me where to find a sweetheart . . ."

"A *what?*" asked the Camel with the Wrinkled Knees, struggling onto his wrinkly knees.

46

"A sweetheart," said the Greedy. "I'm not sure exactly what it means, but an old Chinese fortune cookie told me I would find happiness and never be hungry again if I could only find a sweetheart."

"You have all this stuff around you, and you need a sweetheart as well?" gasped Raggedy Andy.

"Yes," said the Greedy sadly. "I've got everything—cotton candy, chocolate bars and lollipops, ice cream and fudge sauce, butterscotch and nuts to make your mouth water. But—"

"But what?" asked the Camel with the Wrinkled Knees.

"But without a sweetheart, it's no use. It's never enough."

"Oh, dear me," said Raggedy Ann. "I'm really very sorry for you."

"Yes," gurgled the Greedy. "It's a sad case, all right. I've got fruitcake, sugar icing, honey dribbling down my chin. I've got cream puffs and crunchy almonds, but it's just no good."

"Some people are never satisfied," muttered Raggedy Andy, who was beginning to feel a little sick.

"Squash me a banana drowned in jelly, tutti-frutti by the score, marzipan and pastry, caramel and gingerbread galore—none of it's any good, because I have no sweetheart."

"Poor old Greedy," said Raggedy Ann. "That's a very sad story. By the way, my name is Raggedy Ann, and this is my brother, Raggedy Andy, and that is the Camel—"

"—with the Wrinkled Knees," added the Camel, on his feet at last.

"How do you do?" burped the Greedy.

"We fell into your Taffy Pit by mistake. But now we must be on our way," said Raggedy Ann.

48

"Why do you have to leave so soon?" asked the Greedy.

"We have to rescue a friend," said Raggedy Ann.

"From Pirates," said Raggedy Andy. He tried to shift his feet, but they seemed to be stuck fast in the gooey taffy. "Would you please let us go, Mister Greedy?"

"Oh, no, please don't go," said the Greedy. "Please help me find a sweetheart. You have no idea how miserable life can be when you are surrounded entirely by peanut-butter custard and baked Alaska—and no sweetheart."

"I'm sorry, Mister Greedy. I'd really like to help you, but I'm only a little rag doll with a little candy heart, and . . ."

"What did you say?" gulped the Greedy.

"I said I'd like to help you, but I'm only a rag doll . . ."

"With a candy heart?" said the Greedy.

Raggedy Ann nodded.

"If it's a candy heart it must be sweet," said the Greedy, licking his lips. "A real sweetheart."

"I suppose it must be," said Raggedy Ann.

"Well, then, I'd like to have it," said the Greedy.

"It seems to me, Mister Greedy, that you've got quite enough already," said Raggedy Ann, backing away.

"But I told you—it's never enough until I have a sweetheart, and at last I've found one."

"Don't touch one little stitch of that little dolly," said Raggedy Andy.

"Simmer down, sonny," said the Greedy. He plopped a glob of cream on Raggedy Andy's head.

"Don't treat Andy like that!" said the Camel with the Wrinkled Knees, straightening up for a minute.

"I'll treat anyone the way I like," said the Greedy. "It's my Taffy Pit, and I'm going to have that sweetheart for my very own."

49

He produced a pair of scissors from a sticky pocket in his taffy suit.

"Don't you go near that little rag doll!" said the Camel with the Wrinkled Knees.

"Oh, please, Mister Greedy, don't take my candy heart," said Raggedy Ann. She started to run, slipping and sinking into the taffy. *Snip-snap* came the sound of the scissors close behind her.

"You big bully," yelled the Camel with the Wrinkled Knees. He charged, head first, into the Greedy. His head disappeared right into the Greedy's pudding of a body.

The Greedy kept on after Raggedy Ann, who was trying to run. Her feet kept sinking down into the treacly stuff. It was hard to move. Poor Raggedy Ann! She really didn't want to lose her little candy heart. She remembered how, long ago, she had fallen into a paint bucket. The painter's nice mother had washed Raggedy Ann and completely re-stuffed her with nice clean stuffing. Before she stitched Raggedy Ann up, she had sewn in a little candy heart that said on it, "I love you." That was why Raggedy Ann really did love everybody and always wanted to help.

But she was sure she wasn't meant to give up her candy heart to the Greedy.

"Don't worry, Annie," said Raggedy Andy. He was throwing ice-cream snowballs into the Greedy's eyes.

"Stop, stop, I can't see where I'm going!" cried the Greedy.

"Come on, let's run," cried Raggedy Andy. "Camel, get your wrinkled knees out of there."

The Camel with the Wrinkled Knees came out from the Greedy's pudding of a body. "My, that was delicious," he said.

The three ran and stumbled and slithered and slid toward the walls of the Taffy Pit.

"Come back here!" yelled the Greedy. He had a great big pastry tube and was firing vanilla ice cream at them.

"Oh, it's so good," groaned Raggedy Andy.

"Don't give in," said Raggedy Ann. "We've got to keep going."

They were trying to climb the walls of the pit, but there was nothing for them to hang on to. They kept sliding back down to the bottom.

"That's right, come on down, sweetheart," crooned the Greedy.

"Take that!" cried Raggedy Andy. He jumped onto a jelly doughnut, and the red jam squirted into Greedy's face.

"Yum! You throw good stuff," said the Greedy.

Then he started to throw striped candy canes at them. The sticks hit the wall—*thump, thump, thump.*

"A staircase!" cried Raggedy Ann. "Look, now we've got something to hold on to."

Dragging the sagging Camel with the Wrinkled Knees between them, Raggedy Ann and Raggedy Andy slowly climbed the candy-cane ladder, pulling out each cane as they came to it and placing it one notch higher.

"I'll never make it," groaned the Camel with the Wrinkled Knees. "You kids go on without me."

"Never!" said Raggedy Ann. "You're coming with us."

"You can make it," said Raggedy Andy. "Please, please try."

They arrived at a ledge halfway up the wall. With a final heave they managed to get all four of the Camel's legs up. He flopped down with a mighty sigh.

"Look," said Raggedy Andy, "a marshmallow boulder! Come and help me move it over the edge."

Together the three of them pushed and struggled. The boulder began to move. Slowly they rolled it toward the edge, and over it went.

"Hurray!" they shouted.

Down went the marshmallow, picking up speed as it went. Gumdrops and chocolate candies stuck to its sides. It rolled through a patch of raspberry jam. It got bigger by the minute—and it was heading straight for the Greedy.

"Help, help!" he cried. But he was too fat to ooze out of the way in time. The marshmallow hit him right in the face. "Ooh," he groaned, "how delicious! That's a *new* flavor. Oh, yum!"

"Come on, let's go," said Raggedy Andy.

"I do hope he finds a real sweetheart someday," said Raggedy Ann kindly.

# The Loonie Knight

RAGGEDY ANDY PULLED and Raggedy Ann pushed, and at last they got the Camel with the Wrinkled Knees over the top of the cliff.

"My, it's good to be back in the Deep Deep Woods," said Raggedy Ann.

The moonlight was streaming down through the leaves, making ribbons of light amongst the mysterious blue-green shadows. The great trees moved their branches in the gentle breeze, and the leaves whispered to each other.

"Ooof," panted the Camel with the Wrinkled Knees. "May we sit down and rest a little?"

"Yes, let's," said Raggedy Andy.

The three of them flopped down under a tree.

"What an adventure," said Raggedy Ann. "Thank you both for saving me."

"That's what friends are for," said the Camel with the Wrinkled Knees.

"That's right," said Raggedy Andy. "And when we take you home with us, you'll meet lots more friends."

Suddenly the Camel with the Wrinkled Knees stumbled to his feet.

"Listen, there they are again—those beautiful camels in the sky."

"No, no, Mister Camel," said Raggedy Ann.

The two Raggedies held on tightly to the Camel with the Wrinkled Knees.

"You were only dreaming again," said Raggedy Andy. "Come on, we must find Babette before morning. The sooner we all get back to Marcella's playroom, the better."

Raggedy Ann nodded, looking anxiously at the Camel with the Wrinkled Knees.

"Who is Babette? Who is Marcella?" asked the Camel with the Wrinkled Knees, still looking up at the sky, with his eyes going around in circles.

"Babette is a beautiful French doll, and Marcella is a little girl," explained Raggedy Ann.

"Marcella is *home*," said Raggedy Andy. "We all live in Marcella's playroom. But some wicked Pirates stole Babette away. We must find her and bring her back—"

"—or Marcella will be very sad," finished Raggedy Ann.

None of them noticed a pair of large eyes gazing at them through the bushes.

"We're going to do our very best to find Babette before morning," said Raggedy Andy, getting to his feet. "Come on."

The eyes in the bushes rolled. A grinning face appeared, and then some crooked legs. In between, there seemed to be a large tin can.

"Stick 'em up!" said the creature, holding out a gun.

"BANG!" went the gun, and out came a flag that said, YOU NEED HELP!

"You need help!" screeched the tinny-looking man,

laughing wildly. "I bet you want to know where Babette is—am I right?"

"Yes! How did you know that?" gasped Raggedy Ann.

"And who are you, anyway?" asked Raggedy Andy.

"I'm Sir Leonard, the Looniest Knight in the Year," said the tin can, rattling with mirth.

"How do you do?" said Raggedy Ann politely.

"Haw haw haw!" boomed the Loonie Knight.

"I don't see what's so funny," said Raggedy Ann.

"Well, maybe this will help you to see," said the Loonie Knight.

He held a telescope over Raggedy Ann's eye.

"I don't see *anything*," said Raggedy Ann. She took away the telescope, and the Loonie Knight doubled up with laughter.

Raggedy Ann had a black circle around her eye where the telescope had been.

"Hee hee hee, you've got a black eye!" shrieked the Loonie Knight.

"You lay off my sister, Sir Leonard," said Raggedy Andy angrily.

"What's wrong with a little fun?" said the Loonie Knight.

"Fun at the expense of others isn't nice," said Ann.

"Oh, that's *very* funny," giggled the Loonie Knight.

"Stop this craziness," said Raggedy Andy. "We must go and find Babette."

"Of course you must," said the Loonie Knight. "And I'm the very person to help you. Here, have some gum."

Raggedy Andy took the stick of gum, and it snapped on his finger like a mousetrap.

"Ouch!" yelled Raggedy Andy.

"Ho ho ho," laughed the Loonie Knight. "Welcome to Loonieland." He took a banana from his tin-can suit and began peeling it. "Loonieland is where all the practical jokes in the world come from. And guess what? We're going to try them all out on *you!*"

"Come on, let's get out of here," said Raggedy Andy.

He grabbed Raggedy Ann by the hand, and the three of them started to run.

The Loonie Knight threw his banana peel just ahead of Raggedy Andy. And of course Raggedy Andy slipped on it and flopped down.

"Beautiful!" shrieked the Loonie Knight. "I love it! You're in Loonieland; and now that you're in, you'll never get out!"

Raggedy Ann helped Raggedy Andy to his feet. The two little dolls tried to smile, but inside they were not very happy.

"That was a mean thing to do," said Raggedy Ann. "Why are you doing all this to us?"

"For laughs, of course," said the Loonie Knight. "I love you because you are such dear little dollies—you don't know *any* jokes! Ho ho ho! I *love* you, Annie. Here, I'll prove it."

He whipped out a bouquet of flowers and handed it to Raggedy Ann.

"Oh, thank you," she said with a big smile. But as she took the flowers a jet of water squirted all over her. Everybody groaned except the Loonie Knight.

He laughed so hard that tears rolled down his cheeks.

"Now's our chance. Run for it," said Raggedy Andy. "And watch out for the banana peel."

He was too late. The Camel with the Wrinkled Knees skidded and fell, all four wrinkled knees crumpling up beneath him.

"Oh, dear," sighed the Camel with the Wrinkled Knees.

A hole opened up in the forest floor, and all three of them sank down into it.

Dazed, they looked around.

"Look at that great big jukebox!" said Raggedy Ann.

The machine like a jukebox had flashing lights and rolling eyes and it made a funny whirring, clanking sound. But it wasn't a jukebox. Over its huge mouth was a sign that said HA HA HALL.

Suddenly the mouth opened, and out came a long red tongue that looked like a red carpet.

It curled around Raggedy Ann and Raggedy Andy and the Camel with the Wrinkled Knees and lapped them up into its insides. Crazy laughter echoed all around them.

The mouth clanged shut, and suddenly there was silence. In the eerie light there seemed to be no color except the black and white of the tiled floor.

The three dolls clung to each other, terrified.

Suddenly a loudspeaker zoomed out over their heads, like a living thing.

"Attention—attention, guards!" it boomed. "Three suspicious characters are on the loose. Two rag dolls and a blue camel with wrinkled knees. Don't let them get away!"

The voice echoed and re-echoed, and then there was silence.

60

Bravely Raggedy Andy stepped forward onto one of the huge tiles, dragging the other dolls with him.

Immediately the tile shot up into the air, sending the three of them flying and falling through empty space.

They landed in water that rushed them headlong through a tunnel and out through a spigot.

"Heh heh heh!"

They could hear the crazy laughter of the Loonie Knight echoing again all around them.

They landed on the rail of a spiral staircase and went sliding down, faster and faster as it curved down, melting into strange loops and whirls, whizzing up and down like a roller coaster, until suddenly there wasn't any rail at all. They were floating in nothingness.

# King
# Koo Koo

Bump, BUMPETY-BUMP. Bump, bumpety-bump. That was Raggedy Ann and Raggedy Andy, landing.

THUD. That was the Camel with the Wrinkled Knees.

CLANG. That was the Loonie Knight.

"Oh, it's you again," said Raggedy Ann.

"Sshhh!" said the Loonie Knight.

"Why sshhh?" said the Camel with the Wrinkled Knees, trying to get to his feet.

"Because we're in the Court of King Koo Koo, King of the Loonies," whispered the Loonie Knight.

They came to a stop in front of what looked like an enormous tower.

Two lines of trumpeters appeared, one on each side of the tower. They blew their trumpets very loudly.

The tower started to descend, and the Loonies all around the room chorused, "Hail to our glorious King! Hail to our glorious land! Hail glorious everything, but especially, Hail the King! Heh heh heh!"

When King Koo Koo finally appeared, lowered from the ceiling on a large throne, noisemakers and whistles went off. The room was full of cheers and hoots and yells and crazy laughter from the Loonies.

"Hail to the King!"

Raggedy Ann and Raggedy Andy and the Camel with the Wrinkled Knees stared in amazement. The King of the Loonies was a teeny-tiny fellow, about half the size of Raggedy Ann.

*"That's* glorious?" whispered the Camel with the Wrinkled Knees.

"Sshhh," whispered Raggedy Ann. "Don't be rude." Aloud she said, "Please, Your Highness, you've got to help us. You *are* the King, aren't you?"

The Loonies around the throne tittered and giggled. Some of them looked like circus clowns. Some had rubber noses. Some had accordion necks. Not one of them could keep quiet for a minute.

"Silence!" yelled King Koo Koo.

"Please, Your Highness . . . ," began Raggedy Ann.

"You mean Your Lowness, don't you?" snarled King Koo Koo.

"N-no," stuttered Raggedy Ann.

"Yes, you do," said King Koo Koo crossly. "Everybody can see it."

"See what?" said Raggedy Ann, looking down at the angry little King.

"I'M SHORT!" shrieked King Koo Koo.

"You're not so short," said Raggedy Ann gently.

"Yes, I am!" screamed King Koo Koo. "I'm just as short as I can be, and everybody knows it. It isn't easy to be big about things when you're small. And anyway, you can never see over people's heads. How can you be boss when you're short? I want to be tall, *tall*, TALL! I want to be the greatest!"

"Maybe you'll grow," said the Camel with the Wrinkled Knees hopefully.

"Besides, it doesn't matter what you look like outside . . . ," began Raggedy Ann, but King Koo Koo wasn't listening.

"The only time I can grow is when I laugh at other people," said King Koo Koo.

"That's why I have to bring him people he can laugh at," said the Loonie Knight. "That's why *you're* here. Here, shake hands." He thrust out a hand, and Raggedy Andy politely started to shake it. *Wham!* A boxing glove on a spring hit him in the nose.

"Ha ha, that's very funny!" said King Koo Koo. As he laughed one of his ears started to grow bigger.

When he stopped laughing the ear went back to its tiny size.

64

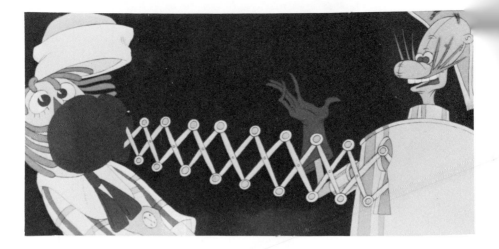

"Did you see that?" whispered the Camel with the Wrinkled Knees.

"Yes," Raggedy Ann whispered back. "I guess that's what he means by having to laugh at other people to grow bigger. Poor thing."

But Raggedy Andy wasn't feeling very kind at that moment.

"Come here and fight, you big tin can," he said to the Loonie Knight.

"No, no, let's be friends," said the Loonie Knight. Again he put out his hand. This time Raggedy Ann stepped forward and took it.

"Ooh!" she cried. A buzzer had gone off and sent a tiny electric shock up her arm.

King Koo Koo jumped up and down on his throne. "Very amusing!" he cried. "I like it." One of his hands grew to enormous size as he laughed.

"Stop that, you bully," Raggedy Andy said to the Loonie Knight.

"Haw haw, better and better," laughed King Koo Koo. Now one of his feet was growing.

"Don't you just love them, Your Majesty?" asked the Loonie Knight, very pleased with himself.

"Yes, yes, they are perfect. They *grow* on me!" He laughed some more at his own joke, and his other foot got bigger.

All the Loonies were cheering and clapping madly. When Raggedy Andy turned to stare at them, the Loonie Knight tickled his neck with a feather.

Surprised, Raggedy Andy jumped about a foot into the air. King Koo Koo laughed so hard his head got to be the size of a balloon.

Raggedy Ann and Raggedy Andy and the Camel with the Wrinkled Knees all stared at King Koo Koo, forgetting to be angry.

"You really do grow bigger when you laugh at other people, don't you?" said Raggedy Andy. "What a way to grow!"

He turned aside in disgust, just in time to get squirted in the face by the Loonie Knight's seltzer bottle.

"Oh, *very* funny," said King Koo Koo. All of him was now beginning to grow. "If only I could laugh all the time, I'd grow to be the king size I'm meant to be!"

The Loonie Knight suddenly appeared with a whole wagonful of cream pies.

*Splot, splot, splot.* He threw one at Raggedy Ann, one at Raggedy Andy, one at the Camel with the Wrinkled Knees.

"Delicious," said the Camel with the Wrinkled Knees.

At this King Koo Koo grew to a truly giant size. He was laughing as if he would never stop. And all the Loonies were laughing with him. They started to throw cream pies at one another, giggling hysterically.

One landed on King Koo Koo's face, and he grew so big it seemed he would blow up like a balloon full of air.

An idea began to form in Raggedy Ann's cottony mind. But this was no time to burst any stitches by thinking too hard about balloons.

"Let's get out of here," she said. "*They* are not going to help us find Babette. They're too crazy."

"That's right," said Raggedy Andy. "Let's leave them laughing. Do you see what I see, over there?"

"It's a sign that says N-TRANCE," said Raggedy Ann.

"In this crazy place it probably means WAY OUT," said the Camel with the Wrinkled Knees.

"Right," said Raggedy Andy. "Just what I was thinking. Let's go."

All three of them dropped down on the cream-spattered floor and started inching their way toward the door.

Cream pies were still landing on their backs, but the Loonies were laughing so much they didn't notice that the three dolls had disappeared.

Suddenly King Koo Koo started to grow smaller. And smaller.

"Oh, oh, *ouch!*" he cried. "What's happening? I'm smaller than *ever!*"

The Loonies, all covered in goo, stopped laughing. Except for a giggle or two here and there, and a yum, yum there and here, there was a terrible silence.

"What have you done, Crackpot?" stormed King Koo Koo. "You have let them escape—the best laughs I ever had!"

The Loonie Knight stood up and looked around in a puzzled way.

"They have gone out through the IN door, you fool," said King Koo Koo. He had sunk way down in his big throne. "But they won't go far," he said after a moment. "Quick, you stupid sardine can, get me my phone. I have an idea."

The Loonie Knight slopped his way as fast as he could through the sea of cream pies. At last he found the telephone and brought it, dripping, to King Koo Koo.

"I will call the Gazooks," said King Koo Koo.

"The Gazooks?" said the Loonie Knight, still giggling feebly.

"Yes," said King Koo Koo. His head grew just a little bigger as he chuckled. "I'm going to have the best laugh of all. It's called the Last Laugh."

He started to push the buttons on the phone with a tiny, gooey finger.

"Hello, that you, Gazooks?"

"Lord of the Deep here," said a watery voice.

"This is King Koo Koo, Gazooks. I have a plan. Now listen carefully . . ."

69

# Captain
# Babette

WHEN RAGGEDY ANN and Raggedy Andy and the Camel with the Wrinkled Knees crawled out through the IN door, they had no idea what they would find. Anything would be a relief from all that crazy laughing and pie throwing. But when Raggedy Ann saw what she did see, her smile got bigger than ever. She almost burst a stitch.

"Just what we need!" she said.

What they saw was a boat. A crazy, mixed-up boat, to be sure, with everything from paddle wheels to funnels to an outboard motor, with hundreds of flags flapping in the breeze. Just what you'd expect in Loonieland. But still, it was a boat. Painted in large letters on its side were the words KOO KOO.

"The King's yacht!" cried Raggedy Andy. "Quick, let's hop aboard."

Hop aboard they did, with Raggedy Andy leading the way up the gangplank.

"How do we get this thing going?" he wondered.

"Well, there are two buttons," said Raggedy Ann. "One says STOP and the other says GO."

"I know!" said the Camel with the Wrinkled Knees. "Press the button that says STOP."

"Of course!" said Raggedy Ann. "In this Loonieland, that's sure to make it go."

Raggedy Andy pressed the STOP button, and yes, indeed, the boat took off with a whir and a clank and a blast of its horn.

"Hurray!" cried Raggedy Andy and the Camel with the Wrinkled Knees. "We're off!"

"Yes, but where to?" wondered Raggedy Ann.

She didn't have long to wonder.

"Ship ahoy!" yelled the Camel with the Wrinkled Knees, falling over in his excitement. "It looks like a Pirate boat!"

"It *is* a Pirate boat," said Raggedy Ann. "It's Captain Contagious. Oh, good! Now we can rescue Babette."

"And bring her back to Marcella," said Raggedy Andy happily.

"Yes, and if the Captain will stop being so silly, perhaps we can bring him back, too," said Raggedy Ann.

As they drew nearer to the Pirates' ship Raggedy Andy put the spyglass to his eye.

"Goodness," he said, "they all seem to be having a lovely time on that ship. They are dancing and running around and it looks as if they are singing."

"Probably naughty nautical songs," sighed Raggedy Ann. "The sooner we get Babette off that ship, the better."

And indeed, there was a lot of naughty nautical fun going on aboard the Pirates' ship—for everyone except Captain Contagious and his parrot Queasy.

Babette had been on board only a few moments after the kidnapping from the playroom before she had completely charmed the Pirates. With starry tears brimming from her lovely blue eyes she explained that she was just a poor, homesick little doll who wanted only to return to her home in Paris, France.

"We will help you!" cried the Pirates.

"No, you won't," said Captain Contagious. "She is my prize, my prisoner. She is mine!"

"Oh, you wicked monster," sobbed Babette.

"Yes, wicked monster," said the Pirates. "Never mind, Babette, we will rescue you. It's a long time since we've had a mutiny."

The wicked Pirates dragged Captain Contagious (and his parrot) down into the deeps of the ship. They locked the Captain in irons, which is what Pirates always do to their prisoners. They even found a tiny pair of chains for Queasy's little feet.

And there the two of them stayed, with only a sputtering candle for light, and only bread and water to feed on.

"Well, at least we have each other," said Captain Contagious gloomily. "Only *you* have remained loyal and true. A-choo!"

"True," echoed the Parrot.

Up on deck the Pirates were having a fine time. They were getting ready to sail for Paris, France. They were not quite sure where it was, but as long as the beautiful Babette was along, they didn't care.

"Topsail rigged!"

"Mainsail jibbed!"

"Man the pumps and oars!"

"Course set! Sails trimmed and mizzened, Captain Babette!"

"I'm proud of you, my hearty lads!" cried Babette. "We'll sing and dance all the way to Paris!"

74

"Hooray!" yelled the Pirates.

Their boots stamped merrily, their black whiskers waggled, and their noses glowed red with joy.

"My, they certainly are having a good time," said the Camel with the Wrinkled Knees as their ship drew closer.

"Why, Babette doesn't seem to be in any trouble at all," said Raggedy Andy.

"She is, she is," cried Raggedy Ann. "We've got to get her back to Marcella. Can't we make this boat go any faster, Andy?"

"There's no other button to push," said Raggedy Andy.

"What about this thing?" said the Camel with the Wrinkled Knees.

He had found a big lever that said on it, DON'T PULL ME!

"We might as well try it," said Raggedy Ann.

Together they all got hold of the lever.

"One, two, three, PULL!"

The lever pulled clean out of its socket. The three dolls fell flat on their backs.

Bells began to ring. Whistles blew. Sirens went off.

And the ship began to sink.

"Oh, dear," sighed Raggedy Ann. "What have we done *now?*"

"It's all right, Annie," said Raggedy Andy. "Hang on to this thing. You too, Camel."

The "thing" was like a tall, skinny catapult. It stayed above water as the rest of the KOO KOO sank below the waves.

In fact it *was* a catapult.

It took aim and fired. The three dolls went flying through the air.

Bump, bumpety-bump. Bump, bumpety-bump. That

75

was Raggedy Ann and Raggedy Andy landing on the deck of the Pirate ship.

THUD. That was the Camel with the Wrinkled Knees.

"Again," he groaned, all his legs tangled up.

"What are *you* doing here?" asked Babette in amazement.

"Oh, Babette, thank goodness you're safe," said Raggedy Ann. "We've come to rescue you and take you home with us."

"Rescue me?" said Babette. "And who—or what—is this?" She pointed to the Camel with the Wrinkled Knees.

"This is our new friend, the Camel—"

"—with the Wrinkled Knees," added the Camel, trying to smooth out his wrinkles.

"Hurry and get your things, dear," said Raggedy Ann. "We've got to get back to Marcella's playroom before morning."

"I will not hurry," said Babette. "I will not go anywhere except back to Paris, France, where I belong."

"Oh," said Raggedy Ann, trying to think. She could feel one of her stitches beginning to burst. "But—where is the Captain?"

"I am the Captain now," said Babette.

"Well, then, where is the Captain, Captain?" asked Raggedy Andy.

"He's down below, in irons, where he deserves to be," said Babette. "Right, me lads?"

"Right, Captain," yelled the Pirates, jumping up and down.

"Seize the prisoners!" cried Captain Babette.

"What are you going to do?" asked Raggedy Andy.

"We are going to hang you from the highest yardarm," said Babette. (She had learned that this is another thing Pirates do to their prisoners.)

76

"But why?" asked Raggedy Ann, as a wicked Pirate started to tie up her arms.

"So that you will be out of the way until we get to Paris," said Babette.

Raggedy Ann and Raggedy Andy looked at each other. They tried to smile, but inside they were not happy at all.

"Never mind, Andy," said Raggedy Ann. "Never mind, Camel. We've all got each other to love. Nothing can happen to us, as long as we're together."

"I know," said Raggedy Andy, as the rope he was tied to reached the top of the yardarm. "But the terrible thing is, we won't get Babette back to Marcella. Poor Marcella!"

"And I'll never have that home, and all those lovely new friends," sobbed the Camel with the Wrinkled Knees, all four feet tied up. "I knew it—I knew it was too good to be true."

"Don't worry, Camel," said Raggedy Ann. "Something is sure to turn up."

And something did.

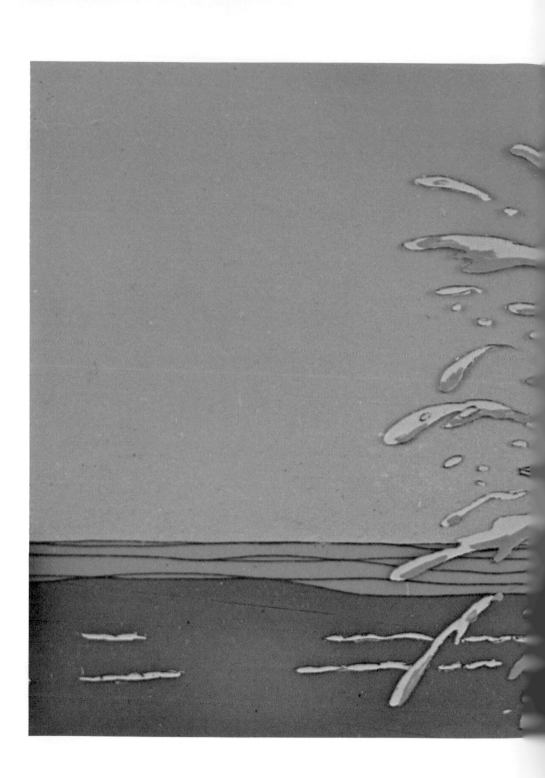

# The Gazooks

THE SOMETHING that turned up was King Koo Koo himself. And the Gazooks.

And a more amazing sight you never did see.

The Gazooks, Lord of the Deep, looked like a cross between a sea monster, an old inner tube, and a great green frog. He was distantly related to an octopus. But he had a hundred arms instead of only eight.

At that moment all the arms were whirring and splashing.

"Full speed ahead!" yelled King Koo Koo. He was holding on to one of the arms, swaying and skimming on a pair of water skis. He was very graceful. After all, it is quite easy to be graceful when you are very, very small. Especially when you are a King.

"Why are those little dollies so important to you, King Koo Koo?" gurgled the Gazooks over his shoulder.

"Because they are simple and sweet! They are the nicest people I ever met! And there is no better laugh than laughing at the really good guys. Ha ha! I feel better already!"

"I see," said the Gazooks, who didn't really see at all. "What is the plan? What are we going to do?"

"We are going to use your talents—all one hundred of them," said King Koo Koo. "You are going to tickle those little dollies until they can't stand it anymore. Hee hee! A hundred tickling tentacles going all at once. Can you imagine anything funnier?"

The little King of the Loonies was beginning to grow at the very thought.

"Not boring, not boring at all," chuckled the Gazooks.

King Koo Koo swung in a wide arc on his skis.

"There they are—straight ahead," yelled King Koo Koo. "Get ready to attack!"

Meanwhile, down in the deep, dark hold of the ship, Captain Contagious and Queasy had stopped being sorry for themselves.

Queasy was busy using his sharp little beak on the lock of his irons. In a moment he was free.

"Good work, Queasy. Now mine."

The Captain's irons were bigger and tougher, but at last they fell off with a clang.

"Now let's get up there and take our ship back!" barked the Captain, moustaches twirling again.

Nimbly he climbed the rope ladder and flung open the hatchway.

"What's going on here?" he shouted.

"Help, help, Captain!" called three little voices.

The Captain looked up and saw Raggedy Ann and Raggedy Andy and the Camel with the Wrinkled Knees swinging helplessly from the top of the yardarm.

"Get us down!" called Raggedy Andy.

"Untie 'em, Queasy."

"Aye, aye, Captain," squawked Queasy. He flew up aloft, and in a trice there was a bumpety-bump, bumpety-bump, THUD! and the three dolls landed safely on deck.

81

"Get back below, you wicked brute," cried Babette. "A-choo! You make me sneeze."

"Can't we be friends, Babette?" asked the Captain. His heart was melting all over again at the sight of the beautiful doll.

But Babette was staring right over his head.

"*Eeeek!*" she screamed. "Look—a sea monster!"

# The Last Laugh

THE GAZOOKS had risen up from the sea, water streaming from his round green face.

King Koo Koo, on water skis, crashed into the side of the Pirate ship.

"Fire one!" screamed King Koo Koo.

A long green tentacle reached out and grabbed the Captain.

"Good," said King Koo Koo, his nose beginning to grow. "Fire two!"

Another tentacle snaked out and got the Camel with the Wrinkled Knees.

"Oh, dear," groaned the Camel with the Wrinkled Knees. "If there's one thing I hate, it's being tickled."

"Hee hee," cried King Koo Koo, beginning to get bigger. "This is the funniest thing I've ever seen. Keep 'em firing, Gazooks!"

The tentacles got Raggedy Andy.

Raggedy Ann grabbed Babette's hand.

"Quick—let's hide in this lifeboat until I think of something to do." She dragged Babette under the tarpaulin cover. Queasy flew in beside them.

King Koo Koo was yelling like the madman that he

was, growing bigger each time a tentacle captured one of the Pirates. Everyone was giggling helplessly, tickled to death.

"Look at me, look at me," shrieked King Koo Koo. "I'm getting bigger and bigger!"

"You see, Babette?" whispered Raggedy Ann. "Marcella told us never to leave the playroom."

"I made a mess of everything," sighed Babette. "What a blow."

"Blow," echoed Queasy.

"Don't let's give up," said Raggedy Ann.

"Up, up," said Queasy.

"What did you say?" said Raggedy Andy as he went whirling past, giggling.

"Blow up," repeated Queasy.

And suddenly Raggedy Ann knew what it was she had been trying to think about. One of her stitches went *pop.*

"Look at the King now," she said. "He's blown up like a balloon. He *is* a balloon! Go and give him a prick, Queasy—he's just full of hot air!"

"Ho ho ho," screamed King Koo Koo. Now he was floating above the ship, an enormous round balloon. Only his head and feet stayed small. "Get the little rag doll! There she is, hiding in the lifeboat."

"This is really great," said the Gazooks, who was enjoying his work. With two tentacles he ripped off the tarpaulin. With another two he grabbed Raggedy Ann and Babette.

"Now tickle them, tickle them!" screamed King Koo Koo. His huge body seemed to fill the entire sky. The galleon looked tiny beneath him.

"Quickly, Queasy," said Raggedy Andy. "Get him!" He gasped for breath, then started to giggle again.

"Oh, wonderful, wonderful," moaned King Koo Koo in ecstasy. "At last I've done it. I've had the Last Laugh. I'm the biggest thing in the world."

He was right, he had had the Last Laugh—*his* last laugh. Queasy streaked up through the air like an arrow. He took aim and dived right into the King's enormous belly.

There was a mighty BANG.

Then there was a great whoosh of air as the balloon-King exploded in a million pieces.

Everybody whirled up into the roaring current of air, holding on to each other, riding on planks, crouching in barrels, clinging to chairs and ropes.

The Gazooks sank with a horrid gurgle.

"Shiver me timbers!" yelled the Captain, moustaches streaming behind him.

"Hang on!" yelled Raggedy Andy, clutching the Camel with the Wrinkled Knees.

"Save me, save me, Raggedy Ann!" screamed Babette.

"Hold on tight!" cried Raggedy Ann.

They all whirled away out of sight and into blackness.

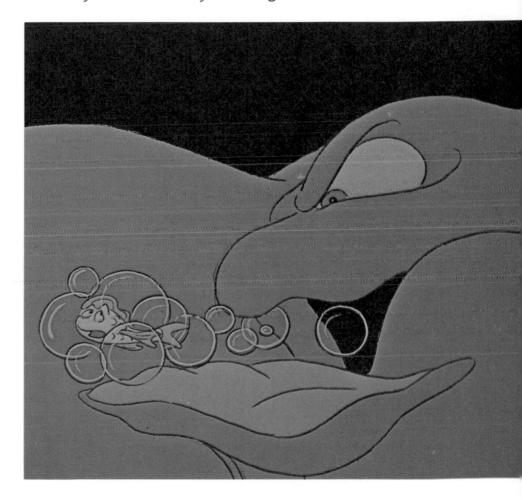

# The Camel
# Finds a Home

Bumpety-bump, bumpety-bump, THUD.

"Ooh," groaned the Camel with the Wrinkled Knees. "Where are we?"

"Sshhh!" said Raggedy Ann. "We've landed in Marcella's back yard, and here she comes."

The dolls froze where they had landed around the edge of the wading pool in Marcella's yard.

Marcella came toward them, her red rubber boots squishing in the mud.

"What are you doing out here?" she asked in amazement. "Why, Raggedy Ann, Andy, how did you ever get out here?"

She picked them up and hugged them.

"Oh, Babette, you too! Just look at your lovely dress, all soiled." She picked up the big doll.

"And Captain! What are *you* doing outside of your glass ball?" As she leaned over to pick up the Captain and his ship, she saw a burst balloon and a dirty, greenish inner tube. "Ugh, what horrid things. I wonder how *they* got here."

She carried her armload toward the house, talking softly to them.

The Camel with the Wrinkled Knees stared after them, only his head poking out from the pile of autumn leaves that lay on top of him.

"All alone again," he moaned, as soon as Marcella was out of sight.

Suddenly he heard, or thought he heard, distant music in the sky.

"Wait for me, wait for me!" he called. He struggled to get to his feet, which were more tangled up than ever.

Somehow he managed it, but by that time he couldn't see the camels in the sky anymore. All he could see was the warm light in Marcella's playroom window. Inch by inch he began to climb up the drainpipe that led to the welcoming light. He pressed his nose against the glass, panting.

"Dear Raggedy Ann," Babette was saying. "I am sorry I caused you so much trouble."

"Oh, that's all right, Babette," said Raggedy Ann.

"We certainly did get into a mess or two," muttered Raggedy Andy.

"You are quite right, Andy," said Babette, turning her blue eyes toward him. "I behaved badly."

Raggedy Ann gave her a hug. "Never mind, Babette. It takes a truly wise person to admit being wrong. And to see that simple things are best. You don't need fancy houses or fancy clothes to be happy. Babette, you are one of the bravest people I have ever met."

"I hope you will be my friend," said Babette.

"Of course I will," said Raggedy Ann. "We all will be your friends, won't we, dollies?"

"A-choo!" sneezed the Captain, back on top of the bookshelf. "I'll always love you, Babette."

"You are a very romantic man, Captain," said Babette. "I forgive you for stealing me away."

"Oh, it's so good to be back," sighed Raggedy Ann.

"And it's great to have you back," said all the dolls. "We really missed you."

"Why, look, Andy, there's the Camel!" said Raggedy Ann. "Come on, let's open the window."

All the dolls piled up to help push open the window. The Camel with the Wrinkled Knees tumbled in.

"Everybody!" said Raggedy Ann. "This is our friend, the Camel—"

"—with the Wrinkled Knees," said the Camel, looking shyly down at his tangled-up, saggy-baggy legs.

"He saved our lives and helped us find Babette," said Raggedy Andy.

"And if it's all right with you, I'd like to have him live here with us, so he can have a real home and never be alone again," said Raggedy Ann.

All the dolls crowded around and helped the Camel with the Wrinkled Knees to his feet.

"Of course, of course," said Maxi. "I'll make some new sticks for his legs."

"I'll sew up his patches," said Susan.

"But we like him just the way he is, don't we, Andy?" said Raggedy Ann.

"Any friend of Raggedy Ann's is a friend of ours," said Grandpa. "Isn't that right, everybody?"

"Oh yes, oh yes!" cried the Twin Dolls together.

"Do you really mean it?" said the Camel with the Wrinkled Knees.

"Of course we do, dear, *dear* Camel," said Raggedy Ann. She and Raggedy Andy both put their arms around the Camel with the Wrinkled Knees and hugged him tight. "And we know that Marcella will love you, too."

"Freeze, everybody, here she comes," said Grandpa, who was in charge of looking out.

"Hello, dollies," said Marcella. "What an adventure you must have had! Now I'll have to see about cleaning you up. Why, Raggedy Ann and Andy, who's this?"

Marcella picked up the wrinkled blue Camel.

"Why, it's a darling Camel—with Wrinkled Knees. Welcome to the playroom, Mister Camel." Tenderly she picked him up, stroking his funny, patched humps and feeling his baggy legs. "Somebody must have loved you a lot, once," said Marcella softly. "And now we're going to love you, aren't we, Raggedies?"

She picked up Raggedy Ann and Raggedy Andy and hugged all three of them in her arms. Just for a moment she was almost sure that she heard three happy sighs.

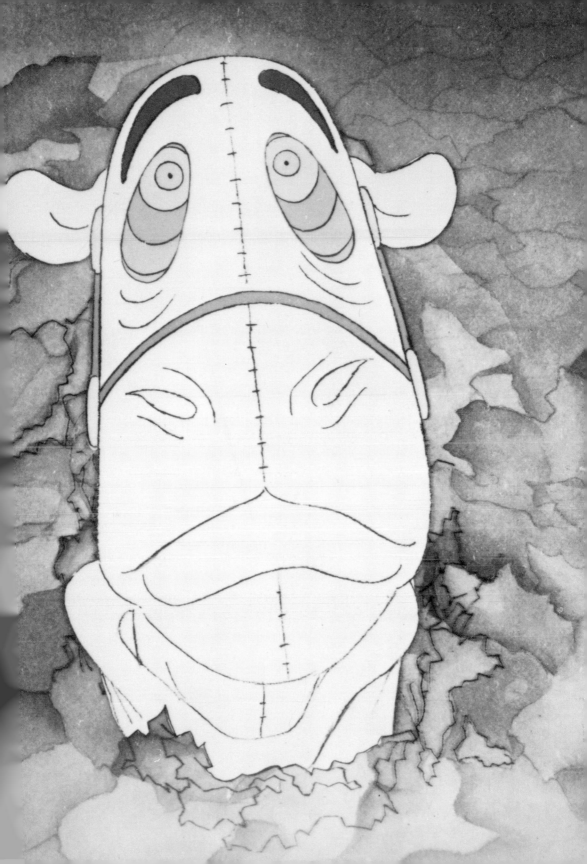